# Fort Ticonderoga

Fort Ticonderoga is located in the Lake Champlain region of upstate New York, midway between Albany and Montréal. The fort (lower right) was "the key to the continent" in the French and Indian War (1754–1763) and the American Revolution (1775–1783) because it controlled the portage between Lakes George (upper left) and Champlain (lower left). These lakes were part of the principal path through the Appalachians into the interior of North America until the 19th century.

POSTCARD HISTORY SERIES

# Fort Ticonderoga

Carl R. Crego

ARCADIA
PUBLISHING

Published by Arcadia Publishing
Charleston, South Carolina

Printed in the United States of America

Library of Congress Catalog Card Number: 2003115047

For all general information contact Arcadia Publishing at:
Telephone 843-853-2070
Fax 843-853-0044
E-mail sales@arcadiapublishing.com
For customer service and orders:
Toll-Free 1-888-313-2665

Visit us on the Internet at www.arcadiapublishing.com

*To my wife, Carol, my daughter, Liz,*
*and my late grandfather, Charles Lewis Kibler.*

The French began the construction of the fort in 1755 and called it Fort Vaudreuil. However, it was referred to as Fort Carillon, a French corruption of the Spanish name Philippe du Fresnoy de Carion, who had Carion's trading post at the portage in the late 17th century. The fort was renamed Ticonderoga, a Mohawk word meaning "the land between the two great waters," after its capture by the British in 1759.

# CONTENTS

Acknowledgments      6

Foreword      7

1.    Champlain's Lake      11

2.    The Wilderness Bastion      15

3.    The Battle of Carillon      25

4.    America's First Victory      43

5.    The-War-in-the-Northern-Department      55

6.    The Northern Tour      73

7.    The Restoration Begins      93

8.    The Restoration Continues      107

# ACKNOWLEDGMENTS

Many people contributed to the successful completion of this project, and I am grateful for the assistance they gave me. Special thanks are due to Eileen Greeley and William Trombley for allowing me to use postcards from their collections. Karl Crannell, public programs coordinator at Fort Ticonderoga, drew the maps of the Champlain Valley, the Garrison Grounds, and the fort that grace the opening pages of this work. Christopher D. Fox, the Anthony D. Pell curator of collections at Fort Ticonderoga, spent many hours with me as I went through the fort's vast holdings of books, scrapbooks, manuscripts, prints, and postcards. He could always locate exactly what I needed. His encyclopedic knowledge of the fort's collections, as well as his eagerness to help, made my research considerably easier. Nicholas Westbrook, director at Fort Ticonderoga, not only wrote the foreword to this book but also wholeheartedly and enthusiastically supported this project from its inception. He read several drafts of the text and made many insightful suggestions for its improvement. The kindness and patience of Pam O'Neil, my editor at Arcadia Publishing during the writing of this book, are gratefully acknowledged.

For consistency, modern names are used to identify locations.

Sarah G. T. and Stephen H. P. Pell, with the financial aid of Sarah's father, Col. Robert Means Thompson, began the restoration of Fort Ticonderoga in March 1909. Since 1931, the Fort Ticonderoga Association, a private not-for-profit educational institution, has continued the Pell family's stewardship of this National Historic Landmark. The fort is open to the public from early May to mid-October and welcomes about 100,000 visitors annually.

# FOREWORD

Travelers have always sought a souvenir, an *aide-mémoire,* a tangible piece of magic to bring back the flood of memories surrounding a travel experience. The ancient Egyptians traveled to the hereafter with a variety of mnemonic tools, as well as necessary food and useful tools to keep in mind and heart the experience of this world.

Tourists—those having the luxury of traveling simply for the pleasure of seeing and experiencing—are a relatively recent historical phenomenon. In this country, tourism was born in the aftermath of the Revolution. Tourists were curious to discover the landscape, history, and commercial promise of the new American republic. New, ever-cheaper modes of transportation, like turnpikes, canals, and eventually railroads, sped travel. Guidebooks helped tourists plan their journeys, steered them to important locations, and helped them understand the significance of the scenes before them. For the creative, diaries and sketchbooks captured the memories. For the less talented (or lazier) tourist, commerce responded with engravings, lithographs, photographs, and stereopticon views. A century ago, postcards became an inexpensive way for tourists to collect and share views. In them we can trace the fascination for historic sites, plaques, monuments, and heroes of the past.

Lake Champlain, and Fort Ticonderoga in particular, offered one of the earliest destinations for tourists in this country. Here was an opportunity to walk a battlefield drenched in blood during at least two wars, to view the romantic ruins of the old French fort, and to see juxtaposed the picturesque farmlands of the lakeshore and the sublime crags of the Adirondack and Green Mountains. Here one could find both the glorious history and landscape of our young country. As a result, there survives a remarkably rich graphic record of the lake and fort.

When one assembles, as Carl Crego has in this delightful book, a century of postcards recording the history of a historic site and its region, one discovers a graphic record of the popular historical imagination. Here we can trace the rise and ebb of public interest in various historic places and heroes along "the warpath of nations." We can also see through a century's postcards a waning public knowledge of the details—even the broad themes—of the wars for empire and liberty that raged through the Champlain Valley for more than two centuries after the arrival of Samuel de Champlain in 1609.

At the same time, each postcard is eloquent testimony, a souvenir, of an ineffable bonding with a historic site. Each postcard proclaims proudly that "I was here," united with past and place. Many cards also emphasize the senders' desire to share that experience: "Wish you were here." The cards record personal links both to those places that are a part of our common heritage, and to others, family and friends, who are our circle of community. Our civic culture, our shared identity as a people, wells up from just such sharing.

Author Carl Crego's collection musters an army of cardboard witnesses to generations of profound experience with these historic sites. He is a collector, donor, and Friend of Fort Ticonderoga. We have appreciated Crego's interest in Fort Ticonderoga, have enjoyed sharing his collector's quest, and have learned much from his new research in preparing this book.

Carl Crego knows—as did the sender of each of these postcards, as did the ancient Greek historian Herodotus—that story is at the heart of history. Each postcard sender tried to share his or her personal story about a connection with the national pageant made by being here. Crego imaginatively uses a century of postcards to help us rediscover four centuries of stories about this lake and this fort.

From Fort Ticonderoga on Lake Champlain, we wish you were here!

—Nicholas Westbrook
Director, Fort Ticonderoga

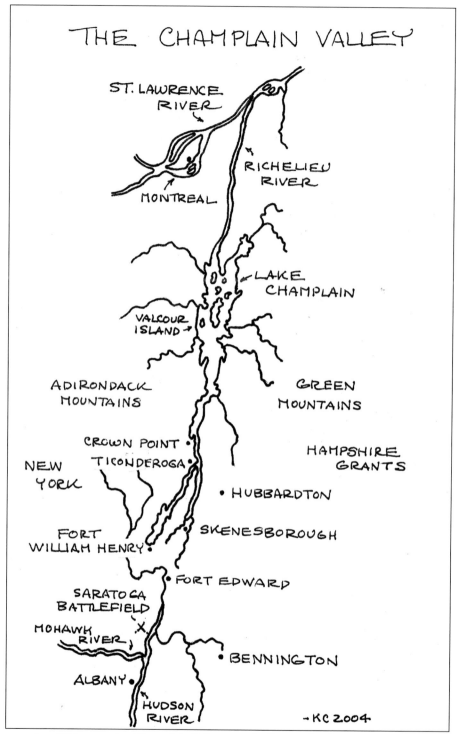

THE CHAMPLAIN VALLEY

ST. LAWRENCE RIVER

MONTREAL

RICHELIEU RIVER

LAKE CHAMPLAIN

VALCOUR ISLAND

ADIRONDACK MOUNTAINS

GREEN MOUNTAINS

CROWN POINT
TICONDEROGA

NEW YORK

HAMPSHIRE GRANTS

• HUBBARDTON

FORT WILLIAM HENRY

SKENESBOROUGH

• FORT EDWARD

SARATOGA BATTLEFIELD

MOHAWK RIVER

• BENNINGTON

ALBANY •

HUDSON RIVER

– KC 2004

For more than 200 years, the Champlain Valley was the "warpath of nations" as first the British and French, and later the Americans and the British, fought each other for control of this vital region.

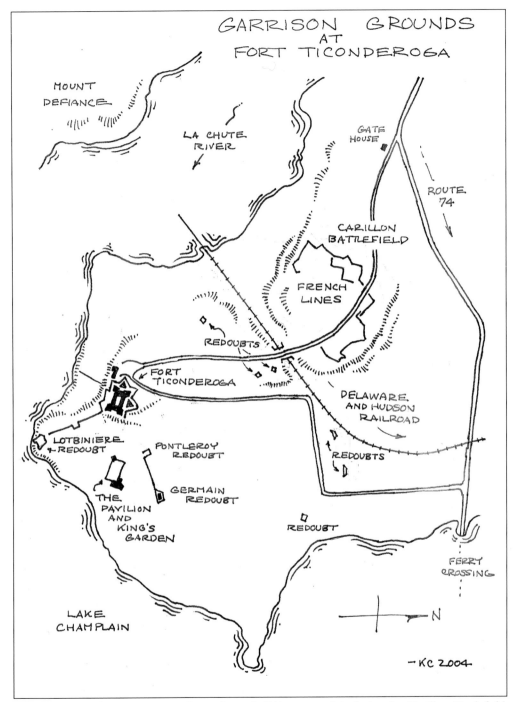

The Fort Ticonderoga Garrison Grounds totals 546 acres and includes the Carillon Battlefield, restored Fort Ticonderoga and its outer redoubts, the Pavilion, and the King's Garden. William Ferris Pell, a New York City importer, purchased the Garrison Grounds in 1820 from its joint owners, Columbia and Union Colleges.

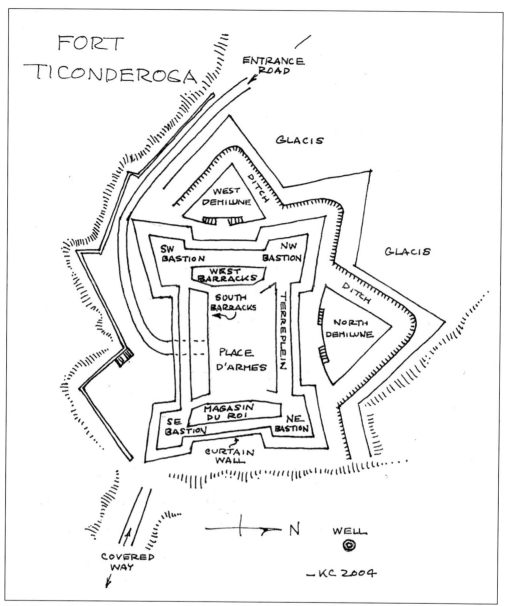

The French began the construction of Fort Ticonderoga in 1755. It was designed and built by Michel Eustace Gaspard, Marquis de Lotbinière, in the four-bastioned style of Maréchal Sébastien Le Prestre de Vauban (1633–1707), King Louis XIV's great military engineer.

# One

# CHAMPLAIN'S LAKE

*I took aim with my arquebus and shot straight at one of
the three chiefs, and with this shot two fell to the ground
[dead] and one of their companions was wounded.*

—Samuel de Champlain, 1613

The Champlain Valley was formed about a million years ago as glaciers moved south from the arctic. About 12,000 years ago, the last of the glaciers melted and formed a saltwater sea. The skeleton of a beluga whale and the fossils of other prehistoric marine life have been found in the Champlain Valley. Gradually, the water flow reversed and the sea became a freshwater lake as its tributaries flushed out the salt water.

For more than 9,000 years prior to the European settlement of the Champlain Valley, Indians hunted, fished, and fought each other for control of the area. By the beginning of the 17th century, the Champlain Valley was contested by the region's two great Indian powers, the Algonquins of the St. Lawrence River region and the Iroquois Confederacy that controlled the lands to the south. Both claimed the game-rich forests surrounding Lake Champlain as their exclusive hunting preserve.

French and British colonists would be drawn into the struggle for this strategic waterway. French settlement of the St. Lawrence River region began in 1535. However, it was not until 1608 that France was able to establish its first permanent settlement at Québec. Its founder and the first governor of New France was Samuel de Champlain.

TER-CENTENARY
OF
QUÉBEC

Samuel de Champlain (1567–1635), French explorer and cartographer, is known as the father of New France for his efforts to establish settlements in the Acadia and St. Lawrence regions of modern Canada. On July 3, 1608, he founded a trading post at the first narrows of the St. Lawrence River. This trading post became the modern city of Québec, the oldest city in the Western Hemisphere north of St. Augustine, Florida. Champlain, like many explorers of the period, wanted to find the Northwest Passage, the shortcut waterway through North America to the Pacific Ocean and the riches of Asia. Although his efforts to find the Northwest Passage failed, Champlain's explorations of the Lake Huron region produced the first accurate maps of the Great Lakes basin, thereby facilitating future French exploration of this area.

CASTLE ST.LOUIS AND CHAMPLAIN, QUÉBEC.

Première Habitation de Québec et Résidence de Mr. Samuel Champlain, 1er Gouverneur.

From his headquarters in Québec, Champlain was able to establish mutually beneficial commercial relations and military alliances with the local Indians. Champlain had heard of a great lake to the south and believed that his only hope of seeing it would be by traveling with a raiding party. He promised to accompany a war party of Hurons, Algonquins, and Montagnais when they traveled south to fight their common enemy, the Iroquois.

DISCOVERY OF LAKE CHAMPLAIN JULY 4TH 1609

DE CHAMPLAIN stands as one of the greatest pioneers and discoverers in a new continent.
THE PRUDENTIAL stands as the Pioneer in Industrial Insurance in America and provides the Best in Life Insurance for Every Member of the Family.

The raiding party of several hundred Indians and 13 French soldiers set out on June 28, 1609. By July 4, only Champlain, two French soldiers, and about 60 Indian allies remained. On that date, they entered a large lake that Champlain named after himself. On the evening of July 29, they came upon 200 Iroquois camped on the Ticonderoga peninsula. Because it was getting dark, both sides agreed to fight the next morning.

On the morning of July 30, 1609, both sides lined up to do battle. Champlain loaded his arquebus, a matchlock musket, with four musket balls. When the battle began, Champlain fired his arquebus, killing two Iroquois chiefs and wounding a third. Champlain's two soldiers then fired their arquebuses. The panic-stricken Iroquois fled with Champlain's Indian allies in hot pursuit. That afternoon, the raiding party began the trek back to Québec.

On May 3, 1912, a memorial to Samuel de Champlain was dedicated at Crown Point, New York. The memorial, which was incorporated into a lighthouse, consists of a statue of Champlain flanked by the statues of an Indian and a French voyageur. Beneath the Champlain statue is a bronze medallion bust by Auguste Rodin called *La France*. The lighthouse was decommissioned in 1926, and the adjoining lighthouse keeper's cottage was torn down.

*Two*

# THE WILDERNESS BASTION

*Fort Carillon, commenced last fall, is situated almost at the head of*
*Lake Champlain. The fort is square with four bastions of which*
*three are in a defensible state. It is [made] of horizontal timbers.*

—Louis Antoine de Bougainville
Montcalm's aide-de-camp,
September 11, 1756

By 1689, Great Britain's colonies were vying with New France for the rich lands of North America. In that year, a series of wars began that eventually determined whether Britain or France would control the continent. The fourth and last of these duels was the French and Indian War (1754–1763), or Seven Years' War, as it was known in Europe (although fighting began in 1754 in North America, formal declarations of war were not made until 1756). This war, which began with a dispute over land in the Ohio Valley, was the first global war, as all the great European powers of the period were involved in the conflict, and its battles were fought not only in North America but also in the Caribbean, Europe, and Asia.

Britain and France knew that control of the Champlain Valley was essential to victory in North America. The French constructed Fort St. Frédéric at Crown Point in 1731 to secure their claim to the upper Champlain region. On April 14, 1755, William Johnson (1715–1774), British superintendent of Indian affairs, was ordered to seize Fort St. Frédéric. By late August, Johnson had assembled 2,500 New England and New York provincials and Indians at the southern end of Lake George. Baron Jean Dieskau (1701–1767), commander of French forces, decided to preempt the British invasion by attacking their supply base at Fort Lyman (later renamed Fort Edward) on the Hudson River, about 12 miles southeast of Johnson's camp.

Dieskau's force, consisting of 1,500 French regulars, Canadian militia, and Indians reached British-controlled territory on September 4, 1755, and spent several days scouting the area. On the morning of September 8, the Battle of Lake George began when Dieskau ambushed 1,200 provincials and Indians commanded by Col. Ephraim Williams about three miles southeast of Lake George. Williams was killed in the ambush (above). The French and their Indian allies pursued the survivors of the ambush to Johnson's camp. As the enemy approached, Johnson ordered the construction of a barricade consisting of wagons and fallen trees (below). After a two-hour battle, the French and Indians retreated. Dieskau was badly wounded during the battle and was captured by the British. In recognition of his victory, Parliament awarded Johnson £5,000 (about $940,000 today), and the King made him a baronet.

The Battle of Lake George was the first major victory of British colonial troops over the French and their Indian allies. After the battle, Johnson began the construction of Fort William Henry near the battlefield. Dieskau's battered soldiers and Indian allies retreated northward via Lake Champlain to the Ticonderoga peninsula. The Marquis de Vaudreuil, the new governor general of New France, ordered the construction of a fort on the peninsula to secure the portage between Lakes George and Champlain and to counter the threat posed by the construction of Fort William Henry, 35 miles to the south. A monument commemorating the Battle of Lake George was erected on the battlefield by the Society of Colonial Wars in the State of New York and dedicated on September 8, 1903. The two bronze figures at the top of the monument represent Mohawk Chief Hendrick and Sir William Johnson. Chief Hendrick was killed along with Colonel Williams in the morning ambush. In 1791, Williams' estate provided the money for a free school that would become Williams College.

**MARQUIS DE LOTBINIERE**

Michel Eustace Gaspard, Marquis de Lotbinière (1723–1799), was born in Canada and studied military engineering in France. In 1755, Lotbinière was ordered to construct a fort at Ticonderoga. The fort was called Fort Vaudreuil, but it was always referred to as Fort Carillon. Lotbinière had no practical experience in fort construction, but he was the nephew-in-law of the colony's governor general, the Marquis de Vaudreuil, and the son-in-law of the late chief engineer of New France. Construction began in October 1755 and continued for three more years. Many French officers criticized Lotbinière for the amount of time it was taking him to construct the fort, as well as his positioning of it on the Ticonderoga peninsula. They called Lotbinière the "Vauban of Canada," a sarcastic comparison to the great 17th-century French fort builder. However, much of this criticism was the result of the disdain held by officers born in France for their Canadian-born counterparts. Lotbinière was made a chevalier of St. Louis and a marquis in 1760. He died from yellow fever in New York City in 1799. (Collection of the Fort Ticonderoga Museum.)

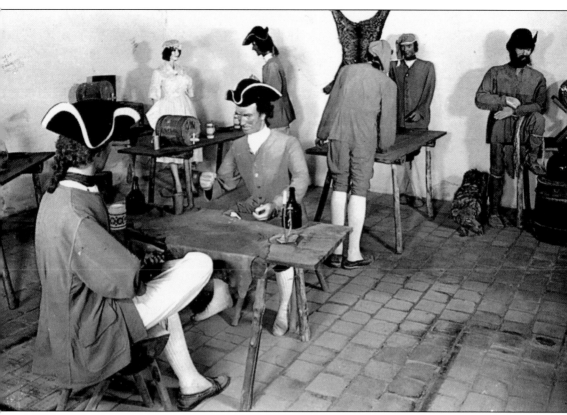

As chief engineer of the construction of Fort Carillon, Lotbinière enjoyed certain accepted perks that enabled him to supplement his income. He certified all expenditures made for the construction of the fort and put some of that money into his own pocket. In addition, he received a percentage of the profits from the common soldiers' canteen. The canteen was the center of a soldier's after duty time in a lonely frontier outpost such as Fort Carillon. Because 2,000 to 4,000 French troops were at Carillon during the summer months, Lotbinière's perks may have totaled several million dollars in current value during the time he was at the fort. This may explain why Lotbinière did not rush the fort's construction despite the prodding of senior French officers. A reconstruction of the French canteen, pictured here, was exhibited at Fort Ticonderoga beginning in 1962. The display was dismantled several years later to make room for new exhibits.

The original Fort Carillon did not look like today's restored stone fortress. At first, each of its four walls consisted of two parallel log walls placed about 10 feet apart. Massive squared logs were stacked horizontally to a height of five to six feet. The space between the interior and exterior log walls was filled with packed dirt and stone debris. The fort's walls were initially made of logs because they were faster to build and were better at deflecting or absorbing the shock of cannon balls than stone walls were. A bastion was placed at each corner of the fort. The baking ovens were lodged in the Northeast Bastion, and the powder magazine was located in the Southeast Bastion. To strengthen the fort's defensive capability, two demilunes, triangle-shaped redoubts, were constructed just beyond the fort's north and west walls, which were the likeliest to be attacked by a land assault. Wooden bridges connected the demilunes to the fort. The barracks for the fort's permanent garrison of about 400 men, the demilunes, and the King's storehouse (*magasin du Roi*) were constructed of stone.

LOWER FALLS, TICONDEROGA, N.Y.

The construction of Fort Carillon required thousands of wood planks that could be made into doors, floorboards, window frames and shutters, bed frames, and other items necessary for the fort. On June 28, 1756, Lotbinière began the construction of a sawmill at the lower falls of the La Chute River, above in a *c.* 1920 postcard, less than two miles from the fort. The river could power the mill throughout the year. When it began operating, the mill was able to make 150 planks per day. The Joseph Dixon Crucible Company of Jersey City, New Jersey, erected a plaque marking the location of the sawmill. The company had a plant near the site of the French sawmill in the present-day village of Ticonderoga. The plaque, pictured below in a *c.* 1912 postcard, was dedicated on July 6, 1909, during the Lake Champlain tercentenary celebration.

GRENADIER'S BATTERY, FORT TICONDEROGA, N. Y.

The Ticonderoga peninsula juts out into Lake Champlain and creates a natural chokepoint for ships sailing on the lake. The Grenadiers', or Lotbinière, Battery was placed at the tip of the peninsula to protect the "French Village," a small settlement that housed the craftsmen, storehouses, and workshops needed to construct the fort and to prevent British ships from sailing farther northward on the lake.

LAKE CHAMPLAIN FROM FORT TICONDEROGA. TICONDEROGA. N. Y.

**MARQUIS DE MONTCALM**
Commander of French Troops
at Ticonderoga in 1758

Louis Joseph, Marquis de Montcalm (1712–1759), began his military career at the age of nine when he was commissioned an ensign in the French army. Montcalm gained significant military experience in the War of Austrian Succession (1740–1748) and was wounded several times. In 1752, he went into semiretirement but was recalled to service when fighting flared up in North America. Montcalm was appointed major general and commander of French forces in New France in May 1756 after Dieskau's capture. Although heavily outnumbered by the British and their Indian allies, Montcalm decided to go on the offensive. On August 14, 1756, he forced the British to surrender the three small forts they were building at Oswego in western New York near Lake Ontario. Montcalm's goal for the 1757 campaign was to drive the British from Fort William Henry at the southern end of Lake George.

SURRENDER OF FORT WILLIAM HENRY, LAKE GEORGE, AUGUST 9, 1757

Colonel Monroe commanded the fort with about 2,200 men. The notable French General Montcalm, with about 6,000 regulars and a Canadian and Indian contingent, in-

Montcalm left Fort Carillon on August 1, 1757, to destroy Fort William Henry. He began the siege of the British fort on August 3. The French constructed siege works and used their artillery to batter the fort's walls. Fort William Henry surrendered on August 9, two days after receiving word that troops at Fort Edward would not be sent to aid them. Montcalm paroled the garrison and allowed them to take their possessions and go to Fort Edward. The Fort William Henry massacre began on the morning of August 10 as the British garrison started its march to Fort Edward. Some of Montcalm's Indians killed several sick British soldiers and then began to loot the wagons containing the possessions of the fort's defenders. Several hundred British soldiers, women, and children were killed, wounded, or taken hostage by the Indians before Montcalm's troops were able to restore order. Fort William Henry was burned to the ground, and Montcalm returned to Fort Carillon. The British were determined to avenge the massacre in 1758 by capturing Fort Carillon.

*Three*

# THE BATTLE OF CARILLON

*They [the Royal Highland Regiment] appeared like roaring*
*lions breaking from their chains: their intrepid courage was rather*
*animated than dampened, by seeing the fallen on every side.*

—An unidentified British lieutenant, July 10, 1758

The 1758 summer campaign, as outlined by British secretary of state William Pitt, called for a three-pronged offensive against the French. The British planned to seize the French forts of Carillon, Duquesne (on the site of modern-day Pittsburgh), and Louisbourg (on Cape Breton). Carillon was the jumping-off point for the British march to Montréal, Duquesne was the gateway to the Ohio Valley, and Louisbourg was the steppingstone for an attack on Québec.

Maj. Gen. James Abercromby (1706–1781), the commander in chief of British forces in North America, led the assault against Fort Carillon. Pitt appointed 34-year-old Brig. Gen. George Augustus, the Viscount Howe (1725–1758), as second in command of the Ticonderoga expedition.

By the end of June 1758, General Abercromby had an army of more than 15,000 regulars, provincials, rangers, and Indians at the southern end of Lake George near the charred ruins of Fort William Henry poised to attack Fort Carillon. It was the largest army ever assembled in North America to that date. Abercromby also had more than 40 artillery pieces to batter down the walls of the fort. French and Indian scouts continually monitored the British buildup and reported its progress to Montcalm. At the same time, Rogers' Rangers harassed the garrison at Fort Carillon and spied on the progress of its construction.

70694 BATTLE OF ROGERS ROCK, LAKE GEORGE, MARCH 1758.

Robert Rogers (1731–1795) commanded rangers who were the eyes of the British army in enemy territory. On March 13, 1758, the Battle on Snowshoes began when Rogers ambushed what he thought was a small French and Indian scouting party about four miles from Fort Carillon. It was, in fact, the advance guard of a large enemy force. The rangers were routed and many of them were killed or captured.

THE ROGERS' ROCK HOTEL AND SLIDE, LAKE GEORGE, N.Y.          H. R. Hulett, Ticonderoga, N.Y.

A legend of the Battle on Snowshoes is that Rogers slid down the 700-foot face of Bald Mountain on to frozen Lake George to escape the pursuing French and Indians. The place where this feat allegedly occurred is now called Rogers Slide, and the mountain's name was changed from Bald Mountain to Rogers Rock.

EMBARKING AT THE HEAD OF LAKE GEORGE OF ABERCROMBIE'S EXPEDITION AGAINST FORT TICONDEROGA

On July 5, 1758, Abercromby's six-mile-long flotilla of over 1,000 bateaux, whaleboats, and barges set out on the 32-mile voyage on Lake George to the Ticonderoga portage. After traveling all night, it reached the portage at 8:00 a.m. on July 6. The entire army disembarked at the portage and unloaded the tons of supplies needed for a 30-day campaign in only two hours. Although the army was only a few miles from Fort Carillon, Lord Howe gave the troops four hours to rest and cook a meal. French lookouts alerted Montcalm that the British had landed.

By 2:00 p.m., the British army began to march to Fort Carillon. Around 4:00 p.m., the British advance guard was ambushed by a French detachment. As Lord Howe moved forward with some light infantry to engage the enemy, he was shot by a French soldier and died instantly. Lord Howe's death paralyzed the army and foreshadowed the disaster that would befall it two days later.

Officer of the **ROYAL ENGINEERS** ~ 1758 ~
Sr. Capt. M. de Pontleroy and Jr. Capt. M. Desandroins of the Royal
Engineers were responsible for the planning and construction of
the entrenched lines for the defense of Fort Carillon, July 8th

On July 6, Montcalm decided to make his stand on the Heights of Carillon, about a half-mile west of the fort. On July 7, just before dawn, Montcalm's force, totaling about 3,500 French regulars, marines, Canadian militia, and Indians began to construct their defensive position. Thick logs were placed horizontally to a height of about six feet. Loopholes were cut into the logs to enable the defenders to fire their muskets from well-protected positions. Small swivel cannons were placed at strategic points along the line to fire shotgun-like charges of musket balls at the attackers. To slow down the attackers and make them easier targets, an abatis, which consisted of sharpened tree limbs pointing toward the enemy, was placed in front of the log wall for a distance of 60 to 80 yards. The French completed the construction of their defensive position in only one day. The zigzag outline of the French position is still visible today.

Early in the morning of July 8, Lt. Matthew Clerk, Abercromby's chief engineer, climbed up the 853-foot-high Mount Defiance to scout for an artillery emplacement at the base of the mountain on the opposite side of the La Chute River from the French log wall. Clerk planned to float artillery down the La Chute River and place his cannons so that their enfilading fire would drive the French from the log wall when the attack began.

THE FRENCH LINES, FORT TICONDEROGA, N.Y.

Around 10:00 a.m., General Abercromby sent an inexperienced military engineer forward to survey the French defensive position. The engineer reported that it was not well constructed and could be taken by direct assault without difficulty. It is likely that the engineer mistook the French advance guards' outpost for the main French defensive position. Based upon the engineer's report, Abercromby ordered his army to move toward the French entrenchments.

The 47th ROYAL CORPS of ARTILLERY ~1758~

Captain of the Royal Corps ~ The guns of Fort Carillon were laid
and fired under the direction of Lt. de Louricourt; July 8, 1758

Between 12:00 and 1:00 p.m., artillerymen in Fort Carillon spotted the British artillery barges being towed down the La Chute River by whaleboats. The British did not know that the fort's artillerymen had already ranged their cannons to fire at boats coming down the river. The cannon shots from the fort sank the first two whaleboats in the procession. In addition, some French troops stationed near the La Chute began to fire their muskets at the artillery flotilla. The French fire was so intense that the British were forced to retreat back up the river. Abercromby's troops would have to attack the French position without artillery support.

THE STORMING OF TICONDEROGA

Abercromby's plan was to attack the log wall at four points simultaneously. This would make it difficult for Montcalm to reinforce an endangered section of the line. At about 1:30 p.m., a New York provincial unit drove back Montcalm's advance guard and rushed to attack the log wall unsupported by the other three attack columns. When the other British columns heard musket fire, they moved forward to assault the French position. Many of the attackers became entangled in the abatis and were cut down by the murderous French musket fire. Some British and provincial units were able to hack their way through the abatis, but they were unable to breach the log wall. The battle lasted for nearly six hours, until it became too dark to continue. Pictured here is Frederick Remington's *The Storming of Ticonderoga* (1897). (Collection of the Fort Ticonderoga Museum.)

THE FAMOUS "BLACK WATCH" REGIMENT AT TICONDEROG⸱ JULY 8, 1758

Of the seven British regular infantry regiments that accompanied Abercromby to Ticonderoga, the 42nd Regiment would become the most famous. The 42nd (Highland or Black Watch) Regiment was raised in 1739 and is still on active service. It is the oldest Highland regiment in the British army. The title Black Watch was derived from the dark colors of its tartan—black, blue, and green—and its initial military assignment to keep watch over the Highlands. During the Battle of Carillon, the regiment made repeated attacks against the French position. The Highlanders hacked through the abatis with their claymores, the large swords they carried. Several Highlanders were able to climb over the wall but were killed inside the French line. Louis Antoine de Bougainville, Montcalm's aide-de-camp, wrote that their charges were the most ferocious made that day. The regiment lost 647 officers and enlisted men killed or wounded out of a total strength of about 1,000. Their casualty rate of nearly 65 percent was the greatest suffered by a British unit on that bloody day.

General
Montcalr
Congratula
his Victori
Troops July
1758,
FORT
TICONDER(
N. Y.

By 6:00 p.m., the fighting was over. Total British losses were 1,944 killed, wounded, or missing, a casualty rate of about 13 percent. French losses totaled 377 killed or wounded, a casualty rate of about 11 percent. After the battle, Montcalm walked among his soldiers and congratulated them for their miraculous victory. Fearing another British attack the next day, French troops remained at the log wall all night. However, Abercromby decided to retreat when French prisoners deceived him by stating that Montcalm would be reinforced shortly with 6,000 French regulars and Canadian militia. The Battle of Carillon was the bloodiest battle fought in North America until the Civil War, and it was the bloodiest day in New York history until the September 11, 2001, terrorist attacks on the World Trade Center.

FORT TICONDEROGA, NEW YORK                4A-H1447

On August 21, Montcalm raised a large, red-painted cross near the log wall to celebrate the victory over the British. Posted on either side of the cross were lead plaques that read, "Quid dux? Quid miles? Quid strata ingenta ligna? En sigum! En victor! Deus hic, Deus ipse triumphat." French and Indian War scholar Francis Parkman translates this inscription, "Soldier and chief and rampart's strength are naught. Behold the conquering cross. It is God the triumph wrought." Since 1909, the year the restored fort opened to the public, a replica of Montcalm's Cross has stood near the spot where Montcalm raised it. The monument in front of the cross was erected in 1927 to commemorate Montcalm's victory.

Wolfe & Montcalm Monument, Quebec.

At the end of 1758, Montcalm returned to Québec, the major city in New France, to prepare it to withstand a British assault expected in the following year. On September 13, 1759, British forces led by Gen. James Wolfe met Montcalm's army on the Plains of Abraham outside Québec. Both Wolfe and Montcalm were mortally wounded during the battle. Wolfe died that day, just after receiving the news that the French had been defeated. Montcalm died early in the morning of September 14. A monument honoring both generals was dedicated in 1927 on the Plains of Abraham.

West Demi-Lune with Three Thirteen-inch French 18th Century Mortars.
In 1759 Sir Jeffrey Amherst Reported Mortar Fire from this Demi-Lune, Fort Ticonderoga, New York

After his bloody defeat at Fort Carillon, Abercromby was relieved of his North American command and was replaced by Gen. Jeffery Amherst. Amherst captured Fort Carillon on July 27, 1759. To concentrate their limited military resources on the defense of Québec, the French made little effort to defend Fort Carillon. Before withdrawing most of their troops under the cover of darkness, the French blew up the fort's powder magazine. The explosion destroyed the Southeast Bastion and the King's storehouse. The fort's South and West Barracks were damaged by debris from the explosion. The barracks were repaired so a British winter garrison could be housed at the fort. Amherst renamed the outpost Fort Ticonderoga. The undated painting below by an unidentified artist is titled *Amherst Takes the Burning Fort.* (Collection of the Fort Ticonderoga Museum.)

Amherst decided to build a larger fort on Lake Champlain at Crown Point, about 15 miles north of Fort Ticonderoga near the ruins of Fort St. Frédéric, which had been abandoned by the French days after they destroyed Fort Carillon. The new fort's official name was His Majesty's Fort at Crown Point, but it was referred to as Fort Amherst. Its Garrison Grounds totaled three and a half square miles, and it was the largest fort constructed by the British in North America. As the battlegrounds shifted northward into Canada, Fort Ticonderoga lost its strategic importance, and only a small garrison was assigned to the post. The Peace of Paris, which ended the war, was signed in 1763. The treaty required France to turn over most of its North American territory to Great Britain. In 1910, the state of New York acquired the land that contains the ruins of the British and French forts at Crown Point.

MONUMENT AT FORT ST. FREDERIC. LAKE CHAMPLAIN. N Y. SHOWING AMMUNITION BINS   84

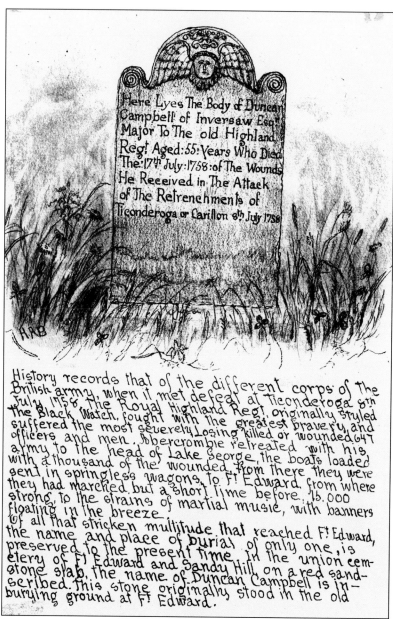

Here Lyes The Body of Duncan Campbell of Inversaw Esqr Major To The old Highland Regt Aged: 55: Years Who Died The: 17th July: 1758: of The Wounds He Received in The Attack of The Retrenchments of Ticonderoga or Carillon 8th July 1758

History records that of the different corps of The British army, when it met defeat at Ticonderoga 8th July 1758, The Royal Highland Regt, originally Styled The Black Watch, fought with the greatest bravery, and suffered the most severely Losing killed or wounded 647 officers and men. Abbercrombie retreated with his army to the head of Lake George, the boats loaded with a thousand of the wounded. from there they were sent in springless wagons, to Ft Edward. from where they had marched but a short time before, 15,000 strong, to the strains of martial music, with banners floating in the breeze. Of all that stricken multitude that reached Ft Edward, the name and place of burial of only one, is preserved to the present time. In the union cemetery of Ft Edward and Sandy Hill, on a red sand-stone slab, the name of Duncan Campbell is in-scribed. This stone originally stood in the old burying ground at Ft Edward.

According to legend, Maj. Duncan Campbell, the second in command of the Black Watch Regiment, inadvertently hid the murderer of his cousin, Donald, in his castle at Inverawe, Scotland. For several nights, Donald's ghost appeared before Campbell and begged him to reveal the killer's hiding place to the authorities. Campbell refused his cousin's request because he had taken a solemn oath on his dirk (a short dagger) that he would not betray the hiding place. The ghost told Campbell that he would not see him again until they met at Ticonderoga. On the day before his regiment was to assault the French position outside Fort Carillon, Campbell was shocked to learn he was now at Ticonderoga. That night, Donald's ghost appeared and told Campbell that he would die during the attack. On the following day, Campbell was mortally wounded. Robert Louis Stevenson wove the legend of Duncan Campbell into his epic poem *Ticonderoga: A Legend of the West Highlands.*

In 1878, Reverend Joseph Cook, a Boston lecturer and Ticonderoga gentleman farmer, placed a small marker near where it was believed Lord Howe was killed. The marker was inscribed, "Near this spot Fell July 6, 1758 In a skirmish preceding Abercrombie's [*sic*] Defeat By Montcalm Lord George Augustus Howe Aged 34 Massachusetts erected a monument to him in Westminster Abbey Ticonderoga places here this Memorial." The marker is now in the Hancock House Museum in Ticonderoga.

A controversy regarding the burial site of Lord Howe began on October 3, 1889, when human remains and a stone tablet inscribed "In Mem. of Lo. Howe Killed Trout Brook" were unearthed in the village of Ticonderoga. Eyewitness accounts and other evidence indicate that Lord Howe was buried in Albany, New York, shortly after his death on July 6, 1758. In July 1900, the remains of the unknown person were reburied in the village under a boulder dedicated to all who fell at Ticonderoga.

The first monument placed at Fort Ticonderoga commemorates the battles on that peninsula in 1609, 1758, and 1759. The boulder and its bronze tablet were erected by the Society of Colonial Wars and dedicated on June 14, 1900. It was originally located outside the main gate to the Garrison Grounds. In 1945, to protect it from vandals, the monument was moved to a safer location inside the Garrison Grounds along the road that leads to the restored fort.

CETTE PLAQUE EST DÉDIÉE
À LA MÉMOIRE DE
MICHEL
MARQUIS DE CHARTIER DE LOTBINIÈRE
CHEVALIER DE SAINT-LOUIS
SEIGNEUR DE HOCQUART ET D'ALAINVILLE
SUR LE LAC CHAMPLAIN
QUI EN QUALITÉ D'INGÉNIEUR ET AGISSANT
SOUS LES INSTRUCTIONS DU
MARQUIS DE VAUDREUIL
GOUVERNEUR GÉNÉRAL
DE LA
NOUVELLE FRANCE
CONSTRUISIT LE FORT CARILLON
1755-1758

HOMMAGE DE LA PROVINCE DE QUEBEC

A plaque honoring the Marquis de Lotbinière was presented to the fort by the province of Québec. The plaque was placed inside the fort on the wall of the South Barracks and dedicated on July 10, 1932. Its inscription reads, "This plaque is dedicated to the memory of Michel, Marquis de Chartier de Lotbinière, Knight of Saint-Louis, Seigneur of Hocquart and Alainville on Lake Champlain, who as engineer in charge, under instructions from Marquis de Vaudreuil, Governor-General of New France, built Fort Carillon, 1756-1758." (Collection of the Fort Ticonderoga Museum.)

On July 8, 1925, a monument honoring the heroism of the Black Watch Regiment and Duncan Campbell was dedicated on the Garrison Grounds. The St. Andrews Society of Glens Falls, New York, erected the monument near where the regiment attacked the French line. Two 18th-century British mortars flank the memorial.

The Scottish Cairn commemorates the Black Watch Regiment's valiant attack against the French line on July 8, 1758. The Black Watch Council of Ticonderoga, the Society of Colonial Wars in the State of New York, and the Society of Colonial Wars in New Jersey erected the cairn in 1997. The cairn is located near where the Highlanders made their famous attack.

*Monument of the French Occupation at Fort Ticonderoga, 1755-1759*

The city of Montréal erected this monument to honor the French regular and colonial troops who were stationed at Fort Carillon from 1755 to 1758, as well as their July 8, 1758, victory over Abercromby's force. The monument was dedicated on September 7, 1939, a week after the start of World War II.

*Monument to the British and Colonial Regiments at Fort Ticonderoga, N. Y. 1758-1759*

This monument commemorates the British and American regiments that served in the battles in the Champlain Valley during the French and Indian War. The Society of Colonial Wars in America presented the bronze tablet to the fort in 1949. It was placed on a stone cairn made of the same local limestone that was used in the fort's construction. The monument was dedicated in 1951.

# *Four*

# AMERICA'S FIRST VICTORY

*Delaplace [Fort Ticonderoga's British commander] had about as much
respect for the "Continental Congress" as [Ethan] Allen had for "Jehovah,"
and they respectfully relied upon and feared powder and ball more than either.*

—Benson J. Lossing, 1850

With Canada in British hands at the end of the French and Indian War, there was no need for two forts on Lake Champlain. Amherst's newly constructed fort near the ruins of Fort St. Frédéric at Crown Point became the main British outpost on the lake. Fort Ticonderoga's log walls began to disintegrate, and no major repairs were made to its buildings.

The American Colonies' relationship with Great Britain also began to deteriorate after the war. The French and Indian War caused Britain's national debt to soar from £30 million in 1753 (about $7.7 billion today) to £140 million in 1763 (about $22.5 billion today). British troops were needed in North America to guard the frontier and to secure the territory that had been wrested from France. Beginning in 1764, Parliament imposed a series of taxes on the American colonies. The tax revenues would be used to reduce the British national debt and to pay a portion of the cost of stationing troops in North America. The Sugar Act (1764) increased the duty on sugar and other imported items, and the Stamp Act (1765) imposed a tax on all printed documents. Pressure was placed on Parliament to abolish the Stamp Act, and it was repealed in 1766. However, on the same day that the Stamp Act was repealed, Parliament passed the Declaratory Act. This act stated that Parliament had full power to enact any law that affected the American colonies. Many colonial leaders began to question their ties with Great Britain.

**SOLDIER
26TH REGIMENT**

In 1772, the 26th Regiment of Foot became responsible for manning the forts at Crown Point and Ticonderoga. The regiment was originally raised in Scotland in 1689 and called the Cameronians in honor of Richard Cameron, a leader of Scottish Protestants who was killed while fighting against King Charles II. It was the only British regiment to have a religious origin. Every man in the regiment carried a Bible, a tradition that lasted until the regiment was disbanded in 1969. In early 1775, its small detachment at Fort Ticonderoga consisted of 2 officers, 2 sergeants, and 42 enlisted men. Many of the enlisted men were invalids or considered to be second-rate soldiers. Also housed inside the crumbling fort were 24 of the soldiers' wives and children.

On April 23, 1773, a chimney fire burned out of control and destroyed most of the Crown Point fort. A detachment of the 26th Regiment of Foot fought the fire for three days before extinguishing it. Most of the detachment relocated to Fort Ticonderoga. In 1774, engineering studies were made of the forts at Ticonderoga and Crown Point to determine where the British garrison should be housed. It was decided to make major repairs to the fire-damaged fort at Crown Point and to station the garrison there. Only minor repairs were to be made to Fort Ticonderoga. The paperwork and requisitions needed to repair the Crown Point fort moved through bureaucratic channels in North America and London so slowly that the American Revolution began before the reconstruction could be started.

Copyright 1905 by the Rotograph Co.

A 6310    Fireplace, Fort Amherst, Lake Champlain, N. Y.

45

Ethan Allen (1738–1789) was born in Litchfield, Connecticut. In 1757, the 19-year-old Allen joined a militia unit that was part of a force being sent to aid the besieged Fort William Henry. The fort surrendered to the French before the relief force arrived, and Allen's militia unit was sent home. In 1769, he moved to Bennington in the Hampshire Grants, now the state of Vermont. As leader of the Green Mountain Boys, Allen fought New York's attempt to annex the grants. New York's royal governor decreed that Allen was an outlaw and offered £60 (about $10,000 today) for his capture. Allen responded by offering £25 (about $4,000 today) for any New York official caught in the grants. Allen offered a lower reward for New Yorkers because he felt they were not worth very much. In the early 1770s, Allen visited Fort Ticonderoga on several occasions. He noted the poor state of both the fort and its garrison. He also saw that the fort had about 100 cannons and mortars and a large store of military supplies.

RUTLAND, VT.                                              4A-H1425

The Green Mountain Boys were Hampshire Grant settlers whose land titles had been issued by New Hampshire. When the British Crown validated New York's claim to the grants and refused to honor the titles given by New Hampshire, the Green Mountain Boys used threats and violence to keep New York officials out of the grants. Their name was derived from the threat made by New York authorities to drive them into the nearby Green Mountains. In 1777, Vermont declared its independence from New York, and the Green Mountain Boys became the army of the republic of Vermont. The army was disbanded when Vermont became the 14th state in 1791. The monument to the Green Mountain Boys was erected by the Daughters of the American Revolution in Rutland, Vermont, and dedicated in 1915.

GENERAL ARNOLD

Benedict Arnold (1741–1801) was born in Norwich, Connecticut, and at the age of 13 was apprenticed to an apothecary. He tried unsuccessfully to enlist in the local militia to fight in the French and Indian War. In 1758, he enlisted in a New York militia unit marching to join Abercromby's expedition against Fort Carillon. However, a friend of the family brought Arnold home before he left for Ticonderoga. In 1759, he joined another militia unit that was heading north to join the British invasion of Canada. Arnold deserted when he found out that his mother was ill. After the war, he became a successful merchant and smuggler. It is likely that his business dealings took him to the Champlain Valley, where he may have observed the poor condition of the forts at Ticonderoga and Crown Point as well as the cannons at each fort. In early 1774, he organized and commanded a Connecticut militia unit called the Governor's Second Company of Foot. This image is a mezzotint dating from 1777. (Collection of the Fort Ticonderoga Museum.)

THE CATAMOUNT TAVERN.
HISTORIC BENNINGTON, VERMONT

After the Battles of Lexington and Concord, Benedict Arnold went to Cambridge, Massachusetts, to get authorization to capture Fort Ticonderoga. On May 3, 1775, he was commissioned a colonel by the Massachusetts Committee of Safety and ordered to enlist up to 400 men to capture the fort. At the same time, the Connecticut Committee of Correspondence also sent men to capture the fort. The militia sent by Connecticut joined up with Ethan Allen and the Green Mountain Boys at the Catamount Tavern in the Hampshire Grants town of Bennington. Allen took command of this group. When Arnold heard that there was another force marching to the fort, he raced ahead of his soldiers and met up with Allen's unit. After some difficult negotiations, Arnold and Allen agreed to share command of the expedition.

Lake Champlain, Larrabees Point and Green Mts., From Fort Ticonderoga Grounds, N.Y.

Very early in the morning of May 10, 1775, Arnold, Allen, and about 200 men arrived on the eastern shore of Lake Champlain near Larabee's Point, less than a mile north of the fort. They were able to seize a large scow and two bateaux traveling down the lake. These boats could hold about 83 men. Arnold, Allen, and 81 men piled into the boats, crossed the lake, and landed on the New York shore just north of the fort.

Arnold and Allen decided to attack the fort before its garrison woke up. As the patriots approached the fort's sally port, a sentry challenged them and attempted to fire his musket. The musket misfired, and the sentry ran into the parade ground shouting for the garrison to turn out. Chasing the sentry, Arnold and Allen raced each other through the sally port and into the fort. (Scene from the Edison Moving Picture Company's *The Capture of Fort Ticonderoga,* filmed at the fort on May 21, 1911.)

Arnold and Allen sprinted across the fort's parade ground to the stairs leading to the second floor of the West Barracks, where the fort's commander, Capt. William Delaplace, and his second in command, Lt. Jocelyn Feltham, had their quarters. Allen reached the door of the officers' quarters first and began banging on the door. (Scene from the Edison Moving Picture Company's *The Capture of Fort Ticonderoga,* filmed at the fort on May 21, 1911.)

A startled, and not quite fully awake, Lieutenant Feltham opened the door. (Scene from the Edison Moving Picture Company's *The Capture of Fort Ticonderoga,* filmed at the fort on May 21, 1911.)

Ethan Allen demanded the surrender of the fort. Feltham wanted to know by whose authority Allen was making that demand. In his 1779 memoir, *A Narrative of Colonel Ethan Allen's Captivity,* Allen recalled that his reply was, "In the name of the Great Jehovah and the Continental Congress." However, historians believe Allen recorded what he wished he had said at that historic moment. Several eyewitnesses remember Allen yelling, "Come out of there, you damned British rat!" and, when challenged, stating that his authority was from the province of Connecticut. Benedict Arnold, who was standing near Allen, reportedly said that his authority was from the Congress at Cambridge. Most observers agree that Allen then told Delaplace that he would kill every one of the garrison's soldiers if the fort was not surrendered immediately. Realizing that his situation was hopeless, Delaplace surrendered the fort to Allen and Arnold. (Scene from the Edison Moving Pictures Company's *The Capture of Fort Ticonderoga,* filmed at the fort on May 21, 1911.)

**ETHAN ALLEN**
Fort Ticonderoga, N. Y.

At the end of the summer of 1775, Ethan Allen joined an American expedition to unite Canada with the 13 rebellious colonies. The British captured Allen near Montréal on September 25, 1775. He was freed in a prisoner exchange on May 6, 1778. After his release, Gen. George Washington commissioned him a lieutenant colonel in the Continental Army and a major general of militia. Allen returned to Vermont, but he did not fight in another battle in the American Revolution. From 1780 until the defeat of the British in 1783 at Yorktown, Virginia, Ethan and his brothers, Levi and Ira, negotiated with Gen. Frederick Haldimand, the British governor general of Canada, for an independent Vermont. Allen died in 1789, two years before Vermont was admitted to the Union.

On June 14, 1900, the Sons of the Revolution in the State of New York dedicated a plaque to "the memory of the gallant band of Patriots led by Colonel Ethan Allen who on the 10th of May 1775 captured this important fortress and secured for the Americans a valuable base of operations in the [*sic*] Lakes George and Champlain." The plaque was placed on the ruin of the West Barracks. Due to Benedict Arnold's subsequent betrayal of the American cause, his name and role in capturing the fort were omitted from the plaque. Many visitors to the fort had their picture taken beneath the Ethan Allen plaque and made into souvenir postcards. After the West Barracks' 1909 restoration, the plaque was remounted on the exact spot where it was hung in 1900. The plaque is now on the exterior of the fort's south curtain wall near the sally port. (Above right, collection of the Fort Ticonderoga Museum.)

*Five*

# THE WAR IN THE NORTHERN DEPARTMENT

*In the northern department they begin to fight. . . . I presume Gates
[the commander of Continental troops] will be so supported that Burgoyne will be
obliged to retreat. He will stop at Ticonderoga, I suppose, for they can maintain posts
although we cannot. I think we shall never defend a post until we shoot a general.*

—John Adams, August 19, 1777

A few hours after Ethan Allen and Benedict Arnold captured Fort Ticonderoga, the Second Continental Congress convened in Philadelphia. Many of its delegates were determined to find a way for the colonies to maintain their rights within the structure of the British empire. When Congress received Allen's report of the capture of Fort Ticonderoga, there was concern that its seizure would enrage Great Britain to the point that no reconciliation would be possible.

Congress decided to prepare for war while trying to find a peaceful solution to the crisis. On June 14, 1775, after a month of agonizing debate, Congress authorized the formation of the Continental Army and the next day appointed George Washington commander of "all the continental forces, raised, or to be raised, for the defense of American liberty." On June 17, while Washington was traveling to Boston from Philadelphia, Gen. Thomas Gage, commander of British forces in Boston, sent 10 companies of infantry across the bay to the Charlestown peninsula to seize the American positions on Breed's Hill and Bunker Hill. Gage's bloody victory failed to lift the siege.

On July 2, Washington arrived at Cambridge and took command of the ragtag militia units that had held the British trapped in Boston since the April 19 battles at Lexington and Concord. He realized that artillery would be needed to force the British out of the city. Col. Henry Knox, a Boston bookseller and amateur military strategist, was dispatched to Fort Ticonderoga to bring its cannons to Boston.

Knox arrived at Fort Ticonderoga on December 5, 1775, and made preparations to transport more than 60 tons of military supplies, including 59 artillery pieces, hundreds of cannon balls, and several tons of gunpowder to Boston. Knox had to move quickly. He needed to get the fort's cannons and military supplies to the southern end of Lake George before it froze. On December 6, Knox began the 300-mile journey to Washington's camp outside Boston. The cannons and military supplies were taken from the fort and loaded onto boats at the Ticonderoga portage for the trip the southern end of Lake George. There the artillery and munitions were packed onto 42 sleds pulled by 80 yoke of oxen and the "noble train of artillery" headed for Albany, New York. On January 4, 1776, the first sleds reached Albany. They then headed east into Massachusetts, traveling on snow-covered roads and paths toward Boston. *The Noble Train of Artillery,* a 1946 oil painting by Tom Lovell, is on permanent loan to the fort from the Dixon Ticonderoga Company.

Among the accidents of the Bombardement was the bursting of Putnam's vaunted mortar „the Congress". March 9.

The mortar was fixed in a bed; old Putnam mounted it, dashed on it a bottle of rum, and gave it the name of Congress.

EVACUATION OF BOSTON. March 18, 1776. The Americans found the works deserted, entered in triumph with drums beating and colours flying. Putnam took command of the city, and the flag of thirteen stripes, the standard of the Union, floated above all the forts.

Fifty days after leaving Fort Ticonderoga, Knox's "noble train of artillery" reached Cambridge, Massachusetts. During the night of March 4, 1776, Washington seized Dorchester Heights, which had a commanding view of the city of Boston, and placed Fort Ticonderoga's artillery on it. When General Gage saw the cannons on the heights, he ordered the evacuation of his forces to Canada. The British army left the city on March 17, and the Continental Army entered Boston the next day.

383—BRITISH CANNON AND PLAQUE AT FORT TICONDEROGA

In 1926 and 1927, New York and Massachusetts placed 56 plaques commemorating the route of the "noble train of artillery" from Fort Ticonderoga to Boston. Called the Knox Trail, it was one of the first heritage trails established in the United States. Knox Trail Plaque No. 1, shown here, is located on the north side of the fort's parade ground.

DEATH OF GEN. MONTGOMERY. Dec. 31, 1775. Battle of Quebec. Within forty paces of the battery, a discharge of grape-shot from a single cannon made a deadly havoc. Montgomery, and Mac Pherson, one of his aides, were killed on the spot. Capt. Cheeseman received a canister shot through the body and fell back a corpse.

No. 15.

In the late summer of 1775, American forces attempted a two-pronged invasion of Canada. Gen. Richard Montgomery led a force northward from Fort Ticonderoga. Col. Benedict Arnold's army traveled through Maine. On December 31, 1775, both American armies attacked Québec. Just as they were about to take the city, Arnold was wounded and Montgomery was killed. After the unsuccessful attack, Arnold began a siege of the city that lasted until May 1776, when the American forces withdrew to Fort Ticonderoga.

STARBOARD GUN AND CARRIAGE ON 1776 GUNDELO FOUND IN LAKE CHAMPLAIN          2900

The British planned to end the rebellion in 1776 by invading New York through the Champlain Valley. That spring, Sir Guy Carleton, governor of Canada, assembled a fleet at the northern end of the lake. Recently promoted Gen. Benedict Arnold supervised the construction of the American ships at Skenesborough (now Whitehall, New York). The ships went to Fort Ticonderoga, about 25 miles to the north, where they were armed with the fort's cannons.

By the fall of 1776, Arnold had a fleet of 15 ships ready for action, consisting of 4 row galleys, 2 schooners, and 8 *gundelos* (gondolas). The gondolas were small, flat-bottomed gunboats, powered by sail and long oars known as sweeps. They were easy to maneuver in Lake Champlain's shallow waters but were difficult to hit because they rode low in the water. Each gondola was 54 feet long. Considering their size, the gondolas were heavily armed with one 12-pounder in the bow and two 9-pounders amidships. These cannons could demast an enemy ship. Several swivel guns were mounted around the gunboat's railing. The swivel guns were used to fire grapeshot at a ship to shred its sails and rigging, repel boarders, and rake the British troop barges. This model of a gondola is in the collection of the Fort Ticonderoga Museum. (Collection of William Trombley.)

*Sergeant of Marines ~ from 1st Penna Bn. Fort Ti. 16 August 1776*

One of Arnold's biggest problems was finding experienced seamen to man his ships. Seasoned sailors detailed from the Royal Navy manned the British ships. Generous bounties were offered to experienced seamen if they would join Arnold's fleet. However, most seamen were making large sums of money as privateers and would not leave the Atlantic ports and journey to Lake Champlain. On July 23, 1776, orders were issued to draft Continental soldiers to serve as sailors and marines in the American fleet. Many of the draftees were stationed at Fort Ticonderoga and came from regiments raised in New Hampshire and Pennsylvania. Commenting on his overall situation, Arnold wrote to David Hawley, the captain of one of his ships, "When you ask for a frigate, they give you a raft. Ask for sailors and they give you tavern waiters. And if you want breeches, they give you a vest."

Arnold ambushed the British fleet on October 11, 1776, near Valcour Island. He forced the British to attack his ships in the narrow, shallow water between the island and the New York shore. During the five-hour battle, two of Arnold's ships, the schooner *Royal Savage* and the gondola *Philadelphia,* were sunk. That night, the surviving American ships sailed silently around the British blockade and retreated south. Two days later, the British caught up with Arnold and severely damaged more of his ships. During the retreat south, Arnold ordered the scuttling of seven ships that were too damaged to continue. Only the galley *Trumbell,* the schooner *Revenge,* the sloop *Enterprise,* and the gondola *New York* made it back to Fort Ticonderoga. The British lost only one gunboat. American casualties were about 60 killed and wounded, while British losses totaled about 40.

The ROYAL SAVAGE, flagship of Benedict Arnold, sunk off southwest end of Valcour Island, Lake Champlain, 1776 (near Plattsburgh, N. Y.)

Carleton set up his headquarters at Crown Point and launched several unsuccessful attacks against Fort Ticonderoga's outer redoubts. In early November, because winter was rapidly approaching, Carleton decided not to begin siege operations against the fort and returned to Canada. The Battle of Valcour Island prevented the British from ending the Revolution in 1776, just months after the signing of the Declaration of Independence.

THE SOUTH PLATFORM IN WINTER, FORT TICONDEROGA, NEW YORK

The winter of 1776–1777 came early to upstate New York. The fort's crumbling barracks could not house the entire American winter garrison, so many soldiers had to live in tents and crude log huts. Smallpox, exposure to the extreme cold, and malnutrition killed many soldiers. Col. Anthony Wayne, commander of the fort's winter garrison, wrote, "We have neither beds or bedding for our sick to lay on or under. . . . The dead & dying laying mingled together in our hospital, or rather house of carnage, is no uncommon sight."

Mount Independence, located east of the fort across Lake Champlain, was better positioned than Fort Ticonderoga to control ships sailing up the lake from the north, and it had a large plateau on its summit that was ideal for the placement of a fort. In early 1777, Lt. Colonel Jeduthan Baldwin began the construction of a large, star-shaped fort on the plateau at the top of the hill.

In the spring of 1777, a floating bridge more than a quarter of a mile long was constructed across the lake, connecting Fort Ticonderoga to the new fort on Mount Independence. Although it was estimated that it would take 10,000 troops to defend the fort and its outer redoubts, Gen. Arthur St. Clair, the fort's commander, had only about 2,500 Continental soldiers and 900 militia, many of them sick, to man the defenses. The postcard shows the floating bridge and the fortifications on Mount Independence.

LAKE CHAMPLAINE, FT TICONDEROGA FROM MT DEFIANCE

GUNNER
ROYAL REGIMENT OF ARTILLERY

In mid-June 1777, Gen. John Burgoyne (1723–1792) and his army of 7,000 British regulars, hired German soldiers, Canadian militia, and Indians launched an invasion of northern New York and reached Fort Ticonderoga on July 1. The next day, St. Clair concentrated his forces by abandoning the outpost at the Ticonderoga portage and the redoubt on Mount Hope. Only the floating bridge, protected by the fort and the fortifications on Mount Independence, remained as an escape route to the south. On July 3, a detachment of Burgoyne's light infantry climbed to the summit of the undefended Mount Defiance, which dominated the fort from the south across the La Chute River. Lt. William Twiss, one of Burgoyne's engineering officers, reconnoitered the position and recommended that artillery be placed on its summit to bombard Fort Ticonderoga and the fortifications on Mount Independence.

On July 4, 1777, Burgoyne's heavy artillery arrived at Ticonderoga. Burgoyne ordered Gen. William Phillips, his second in command and chief artillery officer, to place cannons on the summit of Mount Defiance. Although he realized the difficulty of hauling artillery up the steep, tree-covered hill, Phillips is quoted as saying, "Where a goat can go, a man can go, and where a man can go he can pull a gun up after him." Phillips ordered 400 troops to build a mile-long road up Mount Defiance to its summit. The road was completed in about one day, and artillery was placed on the top of Mount Defiance. (Above, collection of William Trombley.)

Early in the morning of July 5, St. Clair learned that British were moving artillery up Mount Defiance. St. Clair decided to abandon the fort that night under the cover of darkness. St. Clair's plan was to retreat over the floating bridge to Mount Independence and then march about 25 miles south to Skenesborough. As the Americans retreated, one of the huts on Mount Independence caught fire and alerted the British to the American withdrawal. Because the floating bridge had not been destroyed, British troops were able to pursue the fleeing Americans. This c. 1910 view, looking west across Lake Champlain toward Fort Ticonderoga, shows the summit of Mount Independence. The monument on the left, erected by the Hand Cove Chapter of the Daughters of the American Revolution in 1908, honors the unmarked graves of soldiers buried there between 1775 and 1784. (Collection of the Fort Ticonderoga Museum.)

On July 7, 1777, Burgoyne's troops caught up with the retreating Americans' rear guard, commanded by Col. Seth Warner at Hubbardton, Vermont, about 20 miles south of Fort Ticonderoga. After a five-hour battle, Warner was driven back. Warner's delaying action saved the American army, and it was able to continue its march south. The statue honoring Seth Warner was dedicated in 1910 and is near the Bennington Battle Monument in Bennington, Vermont.

ERECTED 1910 IN MEMORY OF COL. SETH WARNER, 404817
PRESENTED BY COL. OLIN SCOTT, BENNINGTON, VT.

The Cannon "Molly Stark" captured from the British by Gen. Stark at Bennington, Vt.

When Burgoyne reached Fort Edward, his army was low on supplies. He dispatched Lt. Col. Friedrich Baum with 900 troops to seize the American supply cache at Bennington, Vermont, about 45 miles to the southeast. On August 16, Gen. John Stark with 1,500 militia attacked Baum about five miles from the town. Before the battle, Stark told his troops, "There are the Red Coats, and they are ours, or this night Molly Stark sleeps a widow." Most of Baum's force were killed or captured, and Burgoyne was denied the supplies he desperately needed.

A raid on Fort Ticonderoga was included in a plan to disrupt Burgoyne's 170-mile-long Canada-to-Fort Edward supply line. The Ticonderoga raiders were to free American prisoners captured at Hubbardton, destroy British supplies, and take the fort if possible. Col. John Brown (1744–1780) and 500 Massachusetts militia were assigned the task of raiding the fort. Early in the morning of September 18, 1777, Brown's force successively assaulted the British posts at the Ticonderoga portage and at the blockhouse on Mount Hope. They progressed all the way to the old French lines outside the fort. Brown freed the American prisoners and destroyed a large quantity of British supplies. A small detachment of Americans also seized Mount Defiance. Brown called upon the fort's commander, Gen. H. Watson Powell, to surrender but Powell refused. For three days, Brown bombarded the fort with several captured cannons. Low on ammunition, Brown withdrew on September 22. (Above, collection of William Trombley.)

Gen. Horatio Gates (1727–1806), commander of the rebels' northern department, decided to make a stand near Saratoga (now Schuylerville), New York, about 36 miles north of Albany. On September 19, 1777, Gates advanced from his entrenched position on Bemis Heights and attacked one of Burgoyne's columns near Freeman's Farm. Burgoyne won the battle, but the northern army, dug in on Bemis Heights, blocked his path to Albany. Burgoyne waited nearly three weeks for reinforcements. With no prospect of reinforcements, his supplies dwindling, and the American army growing stronger, Burgoyne decided that the only chance he had to save his army was to attack. On October 7, as Burgoyne attacked Bemis Heights, the Americans counterattacked and, led by Benedict Arnold, broke the British advance. Nearly 20,000 Continental soldiers surrounded Burgoyne's surviving 6,000 troops. On October 17 Burgoyne surrendered. The Battle of Saratoga is considered to be the turning point of the American Revolution. When word of the American victory reached Europe, France and Spain declared war on Great Britain.

SURRENDER OF BURGOYNE AT SARATOGA - OCT. 17, 1777

1776
1929

THROUGH THIS ENTRANCE TO THE PLACE D'ARMES
OF THE FORT HAVE PASSED

GEORGE WASHINGTON
BENJAMIN FRANKLIN
BENEDICT ARNOLD
HORATIO GATES
ANTHONY WAYNE
ARTHUR ST. CLAIR
HENRY KNOX
PHILIP SCHUYLER
RICHARD MONTGOMERY
THADDEUS KOSCIUSKO

ETHAN ALLEN
SETH WARNER
MAJOR ROBERT ROGERS
THE MARQUIS DE MONTCALM
THE DUC DE LEVIS
SIR JEFFREY AMHERST
SIR GUY CARLETON
MAJOR JOHN ANDRE
SIR JOHN BURGOYNE

AND A HOST OF OTHER GREAT MEN OF OUR HISTORY
YOU WHO TREAD IN THEIR FOOTSTEPS REMEMBER
THEIR GLORY

DONOR
A. STANLEY MILLER

379—PLAQUE AT FORT TICONDEROGA

On November 8, 1777, the British destroyed Fort Ticonderoga and the fortifications on Mount Independence as they withdrew to Canada. Fort Ticonderoga's military role ended. A plaque honoring all the "great men" who served at or visited the fort was dedicated in 1929. This plaque is located just inside the fort's sally port.

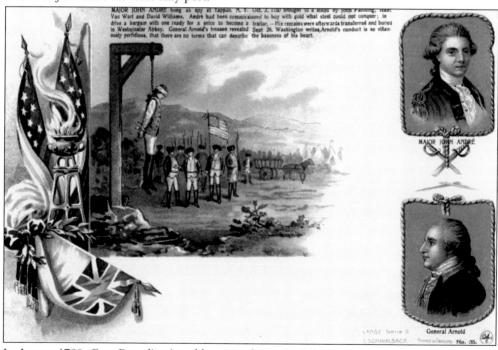

In August 1780, Gen. Benedict Arnold was made commander of the forts at West Point, New York, that guarded this Hudson River chokepoint. He secretly agreed to surrender the forts to the British in return for £40,000 (about $6.5 million today). Maj. John André, chief of the British secret service, was captured with incriminating documents, and the plot was uncovered. Arnold escaped to the British lines. He died in London, nearly penniless, in 1801.

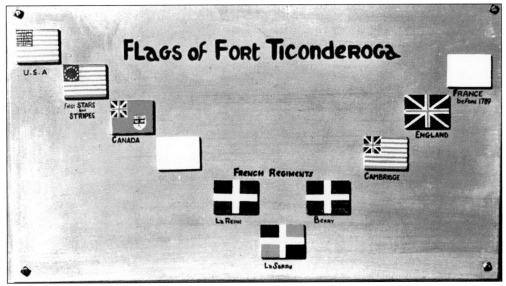

From the start of its construction in 1755 to the end of the Revolution in 1783, the flags of France, Great Britain, the Cambridge Congress, and the United States flew over Fort Ticonderoga. The fort was attacked six times during that period. It was successfully defended against Abercromby (1758), Carleton (1776), and Brown (1777). Amherst (1759), Allen and Arnold (1775), and Burgoyne (1777) succeeded in taking the fort.

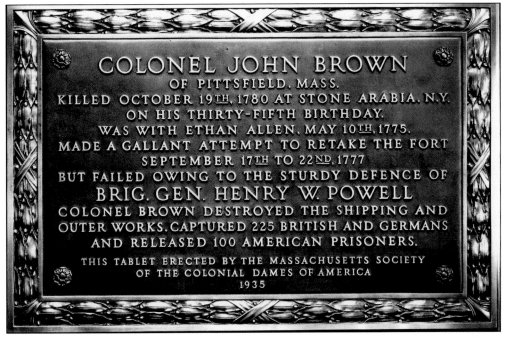

In 1935, the Massachusetts Society of the Colonial Dames of America presented a bronze plaque to Fort Ticonderoga commemorating Col. John Brown's service with Ethan Allen in 1775 and his 1777 raid on the fort. The plaque is mounted on the wall of the covered way that leads visitors to the restored fort. (Collection of the Fort Ticonderoga Museum.)

REMAINS OF BATTLE SHIP REVENGE SUNK AT FORT TICONDEROGA, N. Y. 1775.

In the winter of 1908–1909, the remains of a ship were raised from Lake Champlain near Fort Ticonderoga. At the time, it was identified as the schooner *Revenge,* one of the survivors of Arnold's fleet. More recent research has determined that it was the French and Indian War–era British brig *Duke of Cumberland.* The remains of the brig were crushed in the winter of 1948 when the roof of its display shed collapsed after a heavy snowstorm.

The Battleship "Philadelphia" on Lake Champlain, Ft. Ticonderoga, N. Y. — 21-D-5

In 1935, Lorenzo F. Hagglund, a marine salvage expert, raised the gondola *Philadelphia* and created a floating tourist attraction by placing its remains on a barge and towing it around Lake Champlain. This *c.* 1940 postcard shows the exhibit during one of its many visits to Fort Ticonderoga. In 1961, the Smithsonian Institution purchased the *Philadelphia,* and it is now on display in the National Museum of American History in Washington, D.C.

72

# Six

# The Northern Tour

*Banner would never wave again, nor cannon roar, nor blood be shed,*
*nor trumpet stir up a soldier's heart, in this old fort of Ticonderoga.*
*Tall trees had grown up on its ramparts, since the last garrison marched*
*out, to return no more, or only at some dreamer's summons, gliding from*
*the twilight past to vanish among realities.*

—Nathaniel Hawthorne, February 1836

In 1785, many abandoned British and American forts in New York became the property of the state. On March 31, 1790, the state legislature passed a bill to "set aside the public lands at . . . Fort Ticonderoga with the right to rent or sell and apply the proceeds for the advancement of science and literature." In 1803, the deed to the Fort Ticonderoga Garrison Grounds, which totaled 546 acres and included the crumbling ruins of the old French Fort, was conveyed to Columbia and Union Colleges under the terms of the 1790 legislation.

Military artifacts discovered on the Garrison Grounds suggest that U.S. troops may have camped there during the War of 1812 as they traveled north to repel a British invasion from Canada. After the war, Americans began a voyage of self-discovery, an attempt to find a national identity. Industrialization provided the means by which tourists could venture to more distant places as first steamboats, and later railroads, expedited travel. The completion of the Champlain Canal in 1823, connecting the Hudson River with Lake Champlain, facilitated the Northern Tour—a scenic and historic circular route through the wilderness between New York City, Saratoga, Québec, and Niagara Falls. The romantic ruins of Fort Ticonderoga were a popular stop for Northern Tour travelers.

In the visual arts, the Hudson River school glorified the American wilderness. Its paintings are characterized by vast landscapes in which human beings are portrayed as being in harmony with nature but are small in scale relative to the size of the overall composition.

Thomas Cole (1801–1848) is considered to be the father of the Hudson River school of art. His first signed and dated painting was *Gelyna: A View Near Ticonderoga* (1826). Cole's painting is based on the short story "Gelyna," a love story set against the 1758 British campaign to capture the fort. During a visit to New York, beautiful heiress Gelyna Vandyke met and fell in love with Maj. Edward Rutledge of the Royal American Regiment. They set their wedding day for July 8, 1758. A week before the wedding, Rutledge was ordered to join Abercromby's doomed expedition against Fort Carillon. During the bloody July 8 British attack, Rutledge was severely wounded. His friend, Capt. Herman Cuyler, carried him off the battlefield. Pursued by Montcalm's Indians, Cuyler found a canoe on the bank of the La Chute River and took Rutledge across the river to safety. The next morning Rutledge died. Cole's *Gelyna* depicts Cuyler finding his wounded friend. The painting is in the collection of the Fort Ticonderoga Museum.

Russell Smith (1812–1896), a noted Hudson River school artist, made this oil painting, *Ruins of Fort Ticonderoga,* in 1848. Smith achieved fame for his landscapes of panoramic vistas, as well as stage and curtain designs. Unlike many paintings of the fort made during this era, the topography of this work is so accurate that even today the location from which the artist painted the fort can be identified.

Some Hudson River school artists who painted the ruins of Fort Ticonderoga never actually saw the fort. They copied engravings made by other artists who also probably never visited the fort. As a result, their works are not accurate renditions of the ruins of the fort or of its surrounding vistas. This unsigned and undated painting presents an exaggerated view of the Heights of Carillon.

William Ferris Pell (1779–1840) was a successful New York City importer of mahogany and marble and the grandson of the third (and last) lord of Pelham Manor. Thomas Pell, the first lord of the manor, came to America in 1654 and acquired 50,000 acres that included today's Bronx County and southeastern Westchester County from the local Indians. Thomas Pell named his estate Pelham Manor in honor of his tutor, Pelham Burton. During the American Revolution, the many members of the Pell family remained loyal to the British Crown. The state of New York confiscated their land, and the family was forced to flee to Canada. They returned to New York after the Revolution. In 1820, William Ferris Pell purchased the 546 acres that comprised the Fort Ticonderoga Garrison Grounds from Columbia and Union Colleges for $6,008 (about $93,000 today). Daniel Huntington's 1838 portrait of Pell is in the collection of the Fort Ticonderoga Museum.

The state of New York made no attempt to maintain or preserve the former British and American Revolutionary War–era forts that came under its control in 1785. At Fort Ticonderoga, local residents took everything of practical value from the fort, such as ironwork and roof tiles. Many of the stones used to build the barracks and the demilunes were carted away and used in the construction of settlers' cellars and foundations. After his purchase of the Garrison Grounds in 1820, Pell began the preservation of the crumbling fort to prevent further pillaging. What little of the original fort remained at the beginning of the 20th century, as seen in the *c.* 1908 postcard above and the *c.* 1905 postcard below, was largely due to the commitment of four generations of the Pell family to preserve the fort's ruins. (Above, collection of the Fort Ticonderoga Museum.)

RUINS OF FORT TICONDEROGA, N Y.                    H. R. Hulett, Ticonderoga, N.Y.

In 1820, William Ferris Pell built Beaumont on the Ticonderoga peninsula. The house burned down in 1825 and was replaced during the following year by a Greek Revival–style home that Pell called the Pavilion, pictured above. The name of Pell's new home may have been derived from the Royal Pavilion, the summer home of King George IV in Brighton, England. The Pavilion faces Lake Champlain and is near the site where Champlain and his Indian allies defeated the Iroquois in 1609.

The Greek Revival style of architecture was popular in America from *c.* 1820 to the Civil War. The Pavilion typifies this first uniquely national or American style with its symmetrical shape, low rooflines, pedimented gable, symmetrical windows, and a central portico supported by columns that mimics the entry to an ancient Greek temple. Although the exterior walls of the Pavilion were constructed of wood clapboards, they were painted white to resemble the marble used to build Greek temples. This *c.* 1933 postcard of the Pavilion shows a World War I howitzer to the left of the flagpole and a New York State historical marker commemorating Champlain's battle with the Iroquois to the right of the flagpole.

In this 1839 lithograph, a sketch of the Pavilion was superimposed on an 1818 engraving titled *Carillon and the Ruins of Ticonderoga*. In that year, Archibald Pell (1803–1839), the eldest son of William Ferris Pell, was accidentally killed near the Pavilion as he was firing a cannon saluting his father's arrival from New York. Pell was so devastated by his son's death that he never returned to Ticonderoga. From 1840 to 1898, the Pavilion was rented to a series of entrepreneurs who operated it as a hotel. This new lithograph was used as an advertisement for the hotel. (Collection of the Fort Ticonderoga Museum.)

Hudson River school artist Thomas H. Burridge also borrowed heavily from the 1818 engraving *Carillon and the Ruins of Ticonderoga* to create his undated oil painting *Fort Ticonderoga*. The oil painting is in the collection of the Fort Ticonderoga Museum.

80

New York's first celebration of the centennial of the American Revolution was held at Fort Ticonderoga on May 10, 1875, to commemorate the 100th anniversary of the capture of the fort by Ethan Allen and the Green Mountain Boys. Due to his 1780 treason, Benedict Arnold's role in capturing the fort was ignored. A small crowd gathered at sunrise for a 13-gun salute to the original 13 colonies. As illustrated above in a contemporary engraving, that afternoon military units and bands formed at the Pavilion and marched to the ruins of the fort "along the path made famous by Ethan Allen and his men." The *New York Times* estimated that more than 7,000 people heard the speeches given at the fort. Special trains and steamboats were chartered to bring people to the fort for the day's events. The photograph below shows the crowd gathering to hear the speakers near the ruin of the West Barracks. (Collection of the Fort Ticonderoga Museum.)

As a hotel, the Pavilion had a succession of proprietors and names. By 1868, it was called the Fort Ticonderoga Hotel. In his book *Lake George (Illustrated): A Book of Today* (1875), Adirondack photographer and chronicler Seneca Ray Stoddard reported, "The accommodations are first-class, but limited, the chief business being the dinner provided for excursionists, and for which the house has become celebrated." This *c.* 1890 advertising card was passed out to tourists by Stephen H. Brand, who operated the Fort Ticonderoga Hotel from 1889 to 1893. (Collection of the Fort Ticonderoga Museum.)

This *c.* 1870–1880 stereopticon view by Lucius H. Fillmore, a Ticonderoga photographer, shows tourists at the Pavilion when it was called the Fort Ticonderoga Hotel. Stereo views were popular souvenirs for tourists and were sold individually or in sets. During this period, an individual stereo view cost 25¢ (about $4.03 today), and a set of 12 stereo views sold for $2 (about $32.25 today). (Collection of the Fort Ticonderoga Museum.)

During the French occupation of Fort Carillon (1755–1759), a "covered way," or protected trench, was built from the fort to the Grenadiers' battery at the tip of the Ticonderoga peninsula. Wood pickets placed on both sides of the covered way provided protection from enemy fire. This *c.* 1895 photograph shows tourists walking up the middle of the remnants of the covered way toward the ruins of the fort. (Collection of the Fort Ticonderoga Museum.)

These *c.* 1895 picnickers are enjoying their lunch under the shade of a tree in the middle of the ruins of the "French Village" located below the fort, near the outlet of the La Chute River. (Collection of the Fort Ticonderoga Museum.)

Steamboats began plying the waters of Lake Champlain in 1809. When the Pavilion became a full-time hotel in 1840, a steamboat dock called Fort Ticonderoga Landing was constructed near it. The dock in this *c.* 1875 photograph was constructed in 1865 to accommodate large passenger steamboats. Steamboats moored there for several hours so that passengers could view the fort's ruins and have a meal at the hotel. (Collection of the Fort Ticonderoga Museum.)

MONTCALM LANDING-ON-LAKE CHAMPLAIN. 16.

In 1874, the New York and Canada Railroad extended its track northward from Whitehall to Montcalm Landing at the base of Mount Defiance, about a mile south of Fort Ticonderoga Landing. Montcalm Landing became the terminus for southbound steamboats. As Fort Ticonderoga Landing was no longer a regular steamboat stop, the hotel on the Garrison Grounds closed in 1899. From 1900 to 1908, the Pavilion was leased to Joseph Forcier, a local farmer.

Baldwin Landing, located about five miles south of the fort, was the northern terminus for steamboats traveling on Lake George. Stagecoach operator William G. Baldwin, for whom the landing was named, conveyed passengers between Baldwin Landing on Lake George and first Fort Ticonderoga Landing, and later Montcalm Landing, on Lake Champlain until 1875. In that year, a railroad spur opened that connected Baldwin Landing with Montcalm Landing.

This *c.* 1910 postcard shows visitors going on a sightseeing trip to the fort. Horse-drawn coaches conveyed visitors between the town of Ticonderoga, the railroad station at Addison Junction (changed in 1911 to Fort Ticonderoga), and the fort up to the 1920s. (Collection of the Fort Ticonderoga Museum.)

On May 19, 1898, Congress permitted commercially printed mailing cards to be sent through the U.S. mail at the same 1¢ rate as Post Office Department postcards. This *c.* 1904 private mailing card shows the path leading to the ruin of the West Barracks in the background. In the foreground is the ruin of the West Demi-lune.

Some visitors had their real-photo postcards printed with a decorative frame around the image. This *c.* 1907 postcard shows the ruin of the West Barracks inside a frame that is overlaid with ivy. The ribbon in the upper right has "Ruins of Fort Ticonderoga" printed on it.

This *c.* 1905 postcard shows the remnant of the eastern wall of the fort's South Barracks. This view was one of the most widely known late-19th-century images of the ruins of the fort. Engravings of this wall fragment appeared in *Harper's Weekly,* a very popular illustrated magazine, in 1875, and in John Greenleaf Whittier's *Picturesque America,* one most popular coffee table books of the late 1870s.

This *c.* 1905 postcard shows the northern end of the West Barracks. French soldiers cut thousands of local stones to build it. Thick walls were needed for insulation against the cold winters and to support the weight of the second floor and the roof. The British probably filled in the second-floor window after a 1760 fire almost completely destroyed the officers' quarters in this building. (Collection of the Fort Ticonderoga Museum.)

A German visitor to the fort on June 14, 1905, wrote a friend that it reminded him of the old castles on the Rhine River. In the background is the ruin of the West Barracks. On the left is a fragment of the exterior wall of the South Barracks that faced the fort's parade ground.

An unidentified visitor studies an interior wall of the West Barracks in this September 1909 real-photo postcard. The image on this postcard is one of the last photographs taken of the ruin of the West Barracks before its restoration. In March 1909, the restoration of the West Barracks began under the direction of New York City architect Alfred C. Bossom, who may be the individual taking notes in this postcard. (Collection of the Fort Ticonderoga Museum.)

Vermont, Exterior of Ruins, Fort Ticonderoga.

On occasion, postcards contained errors in their captions. For example, these two *c.* 1907 postcards, one of the exterior of the West Barracks, above, and the other its interior, below, mistakenly place Fort Ticonderoga in Vermont. These postcards were reissued with the word "Vermont" removed.

Vermont, Interior of Ruins, Fort Ticonderoga

According to this *c.* 1905 postcard of the ruin of the West Barracks, Fort Ticonderoga is located on Lake George.

This private mailing card postmarked 1906 erroneously identifies "His Majesty's Fort at Crown Point," often referred to as Fort Amherst, as Fort Ticonderoga. Also note the unique spelling of Ticonderoga as "Ti Conderoga."

State, War and Navy Bldg.

Washington

Secretary of War Taft.

In 1889, 1898, and 1902, bills were introduced into Congress authorizing the purchase of a portion of the Fort Ticonderoga Garrison Grounds and designating it a national park. The bills died in committee. In 1890, Congress directed the War Department to conserve historic battlefields and forts as national military parks. In late 1905, the Ticonderoga Historical Society, formed in 1897, appealed to Secretary of War William Howard Taft (1857–1930) to request an appropriation from Congress to purchase the Garrison Grounds and to designate it a national military park. On February 11, 1906, Taft responded that it would be impossible to make the funding request for Fort Ticonderoga because "there are too many calls upon Congress" for money. On February 13, 1906, HR 14805 was introduced in another attempt to purchase the fort and to establish a national park on the Garrison Grounds. This bill also died in committee. Ironically, as the newly inaugurated president of the United States, Taft visited Fort Ticonderoga on July 6, 1909, to celebrate opening day of the restored West Barracks.

CLAM BAKE AT FORT TICONDEROGA, N.Y. SEPT. 2nd 1908.

On September 2, 1908, the Ticonderoga Historical Society hosted a clambake at the Pavilion for the members of the Champlain Valley press corps to win their support for yet another attempt to introduce congressional legislation authorizing the purchase the Fort Ticonderoga Garrison Grounds. At the clambake, New York City architect Alfred C. Bossom presented his plans for the restoration of the fort. Among those in attendance was Wall Street financier Stephen Hyatt Pelham Pell, the great-grandson of William Ferris Pell. This was Pell's first visit to Ticonderoga in 25 years, and he was dismayed by the deterioration of the fort during that period. He decided to talk to his wife, Sarah Gibbs Thompson Pell, and his wealthy father-in-law, Col. Robert Means Thompson, about restoring the fort. These postcards show spectators listening to presentations being made by members of the Ticonderoga Historical Society during the clambake. (Below, collection of the Fort Ticonderoga Museum.)

*Seven*

# THE RESTORATION BEGINS

*Why not? Have it done [the restoration of Fort Ticonderoga] and send the bill to me.*

—Col. Robert Means Thompson, 1908

Long before the 1908 Ticonderoga Historical Society's clambake, Stephen Pell had a desire to restore Fort Ticonderoga. According to family lore, in the summer of 1883 eight-year-old Stephen and his older brother traveled to Ticonderoga to visit their grandmother who was staying at the Fort Ticonderoga Hotel (the Pavilion). As the boys were playing in the ruins of the fort, the older brother dislodged a stone, and Stephen found a bronze flint box under it. This discovery started Stephen's lifelong interest in restoring the old French fort.

Immediately after the clambake, Stephen Pell began to make plans to rebuild the fort. His father-in-law, Col. Robert Means Thompson, pledged $500,000 (about $9.5 million today) to fund the project. Architect Alfred C. Bossom was hired to oversee the restoration. They planned to have the West Barracks, where Ethan Allen and Benedict Arnold demanded the surrender of the fort from its British commander, restored by July 6, 1909, the date of the Champlain tercentenary celebration at Ticonderoga. The celebration was a seven-day event (July 4 through July 10) hosted by New York and Vermont to commemorate the exploration of the region by Samuel de Champlain in 1609.

Before any restoration work could begin, however, Stephen Pell had to purchase the shares of the Garrison Grounds held by other family members. It took Pell until mid-November to secure these shares, and by then, it was too late in the season to begin the restoration. Work on the West Barracks began in the spring of 1909.

Stephen H. P. Pell (1874–1950) served on the auxiliary cruiser USS *Yankee* and saw action at the naval Battle of Santiago during the Spanish-American War (1898). In 1899, he formed S. H. P. Pell & Company, a New York City coffee, cotton, and stock brokerage firm. In early 1917, Pell enlisted in the French army but was transferred to the American army's ambulance corps after the United States entered World War I later that year. He was wounded in action on August 3, 1918. In 1927, Pell was awarded the Legion of Honor by the government of France in recognition of his service to that country in World War I and for the restoration of Fort Ticonderoga. Until his death in 1950, Pell dedicated himself to the restoration of fort and to expanding the museum's collections. He is buried in the family plot near the Pavilion and his beloved fort. This photograph of Pell was taken *c.* 1929. (Collection of the Fort Ticonderoga Museum.)

Sarah Gibbs Thompson Pell (1878–1939), daughter of Robert Means Thompson, studied music in Paris prior to her 1901 marriage to Stephen H. P. Pell. During a trip to England, she met Mrs. Emmeline Pankhurst, a leader of the British suffrage movement. This meeting instilled in Sarah a lifelong interest in the women's rights movement. Sarah believed that women needed more than the right to vote, as provided by the Nineteenth Amendment, to secure equal rights. To this end, Sarah served as the national chair of the National Women's Party during the 1920s. The party's key platform was the passage of a constitutional amendment that would grant equal rights to women. Sarah was also active in the Republican party in New York. She used her social and political connections to lobby Presidents Coolidge and Hoover for an equal rights amendment. This photograph of Sarah G. T. Pell was taken around the time of her wedding to Stephen Pell. (Collection of the Fort Ticonderoga Museum.)

Robert Means Thompson (1849–1930) was the son of a lay judge in Jefferson County, Pennsylvania. He served in the navy for three years after his graduation from the U.S. Naval Academy in 1868. Thompson graduated from Harvard Law School in 1874. Although he had a naval background, Thompson was known as "the Colonel," the rank he received while serving on the staff of the governor of New Jersey. In 1902, with the aid of the Rothchilds, he consolidated small nickel-mining companies into the International Nickel Company. For a time, the International Nickel Company controlled the world's output of that metal. Thompson and his brother-in-law donated the money to fund the Thompson Cup, the trophy given to the winner of the annual Army-Navy football game. The Naval Academy's football field was named Thompson Field in honor of his contributions to the school. He also served as chairman of the American Olympic Committee for the 1912 and 1924 Olympic Games. (Collection of the Fort Ticonderoga Museum.)

Alfred Charles, Lord Bossom of Maidstone (1881–1965), baronet, was educated at the Royal Academy of Arts in London and came to the United States in 1903. The next year, he made his first visit to Ticonderoga. Bossom admired the ruins of the fort and became interested in its restoration. He served as the architect for the fort's restoration from 1908 to *c.* 1914. While in the United States, Bossom designed more than 50 skyscrapers, including the Seaboard National Bank Building in New York City, which won an architectural prize. Ironically, Bossom believed that "architecture should be a portrait in brick and stone of the type of life led by the people within its walls and we [the English] are not a skyscraper nation." After his return to England in late 1926, Bossom joined the Conservative party and was elected to Parliament in 1931. He was given a baronetcy in 1953 and was named a life peer in 1960 for his political and public services. This picture of Lord Bossom was taken in 1962 during his last visit to the fort. (Collection of the Fort Ticonderoga Museum.)

After his first visit to Fort Ticonderoga in 1904, Bossom became interested in restoring the fort. Encouraged by John E. Milholland, the former owner-editor of the local newspaper, the *Ticonderoga Sentinel,* Bossom combed libraries in the United States, Great Britain, France, and Canada for information regarding Fort Carillon-Ticonderoga's design and construction. As his research continued, his designs for the restored fort changed. In the *c.* 1909 postcard above, the fort's South Barracks, to the right of the tall tower, are pictured as two buildings separated by the fort's sally port. In a later undated drawing, below, the South Barracks, to the left of the tower, is portrayed as one building and was restored in 1931 as one building. There is no archaeological or documentary evidence supporting the tower that Bossom included in his vision of the restored fort. (Above, collection of William Trombley; below, collection of the Fort Ticonderoga Museum.)

THE PAVILION, RESIDENCE OF S. H. P. PELL, ESQ., FORT TICONDEROGA, N. Y

The Pell family decided to repair the Pavilion so that they could use it as a summer home. The Pavilion had been used most recently as a farmhouse but had been neglected by its tenants for more than a decade. Work on the interior of the Pavilion began in the late fall of 1908 and continued through the winter. In a February 9, 1909, letter to his mother, Stephen Pell wrote, "We are pushing the work on the old house at Ticonderoga and it will be finished by the Spring. We are [re]building an extension in the rear and putting in plumbing, which formerly did not exist.... We took down all of the plaster, took up all the floors, put on a new roof and added five fire-places. So the house will look exactly as it did in the old days, but everything we come in contact with will be new. This is rather necessary as there was a cow in the parlor the last time I was in Ticonderoga." The rear extension to the Pavilion can be seen below.

The King's Garden (Le Jardin du Roi) 1755
Fort Ticonderoga, New York

The restoration of the West Barracks began on March 29, 1909. This postcard is the earliest known photograph of the start of the restoration of the West Barracks. The undergrowth has been cleared from inside the barracks, and stones are piled up to be used for the restoration of the walls. The caption at the bottom left of the postcard says, "Officers Headquarters Excavated."

By early May 1909, about 40 days after the start of the reconstruction of the West Barracks, its exterior walls were repaired up to the second story, and the framing of the first floor interior walls had started. The small shack on the left was the office of architect Alfred C. Bossom and construction contractor William A. Gale. (Collection of the Essex County Historical Society.)

On May 5, 1909, the members of the Lake Champlain Tercentenary Commission visited the fort to inspect the progress being made on the restoration of the West Barracks and to select sites on the Garrison Grounds for the July 6 tercentenary festivities at Ticonderoga. The construction crew working on the West Barracks had been recently expanded from 20 to about 100 carpenters and masons. (Collection of the Essex County Historical Society.)

By July 6, 1909, 100 days after the start of the reconstruction, the exterior walls of the West Barracks had been completely restored and a temporary roof installed. However, there was no glass in the windows and no tiles on the roof. Bossom was unable to find American manufacturers who could make reproductions of 18th-century window glass or roof tiles. English manufacturers were eventually located to create these items, and orders were placed with them in mid-June.

Although a heavy rain fell on the morning of July 6, 1909, hundreds of people came to the fort to see the West Barracks and to view the artifacts recovered during its restoration. Work on the West Barracks continued for the next three years.

Pres. William Howard Taft attended the Lake Champlain tercentenary celebration at Ticonderoga on July 6. Inspecting the restoration work being done on the fort are, from left to right, the following: Stephen H. P. Pell, Sarah G. T. Pell, President Taft, Capt. William Butts (the president's military aide), and Alfred C. Bossom. (Collection of the Essex County Historical Society.)

President Taft and Bossom review the plans for the restoration of the fort and the French village. The president also viewed the thousands of artifacts, including more than 200 cannon balls that were discovered during the restoration of the West Barracks. (Collection of the Fort Ticonderoga Museum.)

PRESIDENT TAFT AT FORT TICONDEROGA, JULY, 1909.

President Taft leaves the fort to be taken by car to the speakers' platform. Seen, from left to right, are the following: an unidentified New York National Guard soldier, David Williams (publisher of the magazine *Iron Age* and owner of the nearby Rogers Rock Hotel), President Taft, Alfred C. Bossom, and Sarah G. T. Pell.

103

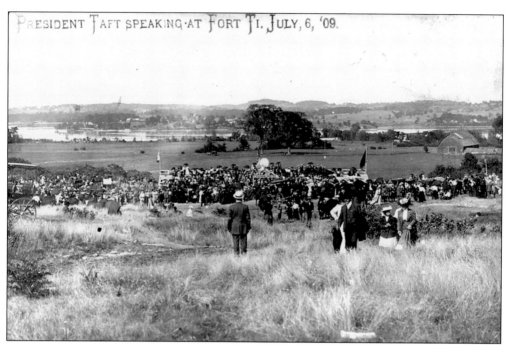

More than 1,000 people gathered at the speaker's platform set up below the Heights of Carillon, near the shore of Lake Champlain, to hear the Ticonderoga tercentenary celebration speeches.

As President Taft was being driven to the speakers' platform, his car went into a skid as it traveled down the steep, rain-soaked, muddy road that linked the restored fort on the Heights of Carillon to the speakers' platform. The chauffeur got the car under control before it went off the road and averted a serious accident. Sitting next to the president is Howland Pell, a cousin of Stephen Pell. (Collection of the Essex County Historical Society.)

President Taft, standing near the center of the speakers' platform, gave a brief speech in which he appealed for peace among all nations. New York governor Charles E. Hughes, Vermont governor George H. Prouty, British ambassador Rt. Hon. James Bryce, and French ambassador Jean Jules Jusserand were among the many dignitaries who attended the Ticonderoga tercentenary celebration and viewed the progress of the restoration of the West Barracks. (Collection of the Fort Ticonderoga Museum.)

After delivering his speech, President Taft went to the Pavilion to have afternoon tea with the Pell family and invited guests. Standing on the lower front step of the Pavilion are, from left to right, Sarah G. T. Pell, President Taft, and Stephen H. P. Pell. In the background, between the president and Stephen Pell, is Col. Robert Means Thompson. (Collection of the Fort Ticonderoga Museum.)

An Indian pageant consisting of portrayals of Champlain's 1609 battle with the Iroquois and Longfellow's poem, *Hiawatha,* was presented at towns along the shore of Lake Champlain during the Ticonderoga tercentenary celebration. Several barges were tied together and covered with earth, rocks, and trees to create a stage. The background scenery consisted of a stockade, wigwams, and teepees. Nearly 150 Indians participated in the two plays. For the Ticonderoga performance, given on July 6, the floating stage was anchored near the fort. (Above, collection of the Fort Ticonderoga Museum.)

# *Eight*

# THE RESTORATION

# CONTINUES

*We have been criticized in some of the newspapers for undertaking
the restoration at all; but when I saw the ruins as they stood in 1908 and
as I remembered them in 1883, I was impressed with the fact that
in another quarter of a century there would be little left to show.*

—Stephen H. P. Pell, 1912

The restoration of the West Barracks was only the first phase of the Pell family's Fort Ticonderoga project. The reconstruction of the South Barracks began in early 1914, but it was stopped temporarily on Friday July 31, 1914. On that day, Stephen Pell's brokerage firm was forced into receivership when cotton prices collapsed due to market uncertainties regarding the outbreak of war in Europe (World War I began on July 28). Pell had made a large fortune by betting on ever increasing cotton prices. However, when the price of cotton collapsed on that black Friday, his company had net liabilities of more than $1.5 million (about $27.6 million today). By the time his firm's financial affairs were resolved, America had entered World War I, and building materials not required for the war effort were very expensive.

After Pell's return from World War I in 1919, the restoration of the fort resumed. By 1922, the financial burden of maintaining the Garrison Grounds, adding to the fort's collection, and accommodating increasing numbers of tourists became such that Pell initiated an admission charge of 50¢ (about $5.60 today) to defray these costs.

To ensure the continued restoration and preservation of the fort, the Pell family formed a not-for-profit educational institution, the Fort Ticonderoga Association, in 1931. Today, the association cares for more than 2,000 acres of historically significant land in New York and Vermont, as well as a world-class collection of 18th-century military objects and archives.

In 1909, Bossom designed a summer home for Howland Pell that was constructed north of the Pavilion inside the Germain Redoubt. Completed in 1910, Pell's home was built on the foundation of a blockhouse built by the French in 1758, and it was informally known by that name. In the late 1920s and again in the 1940s, it served as a temporary location for the fort's library. The Blockhouse is not open to the public.

The Gatehouse, also designed by Bossom, replicates, on a smaller scale, the exterior of the restored West Barracks. Constructed between 1909 and 1910, its exterior walls are constructed of the same type of stone that was used to build the fort's barracks and demilunes. The Gatehouse has been a private residence since its construction and is not open to the public.

Although its official opening day was July 6, 1909, work on the West Barracks continued over the next three years. In the *c.* 1911 postcard above, the roof is still only partially tiled and there are no dormers. By 1912, as shown below, the roof had been completely tiled and the dormers had been constructed. The only significant change made to the exterior of the West Barracks was made in the late 1920s, when multiple staircases replaced the external single staircase and the long porch outside the second floor.

Until the second floor of the West Barracks was completed in 1910, the fort's collection of artifacts was on display in the restored ground floor. The triangular cases on top of the long tables contained artifacts collected during the barracks' restoration. Hanging on the wall to the left in the background are ax heads found at the fort.

Around 1951, the fort's collection of weaponry, consisting of more than 100 muskets, rifles, swords, and other weapons dating from 1650 to 1820, was moved to the ground floor of the West Barracks. The fort has one of the largest and most comprehensive collections of British, French, German, and American 18th-century military firearms used in the colonial wars.

THE FRENCH ROOM, FORT TICONDEROGA, N. Y.

From 1910 until the opening of the newly restored South Barracks in 1931, the second floor of the West Barracks was the main display area for the fort's growing collection of 18th-century firearms, artifacts, and documents. As can be seen in these two *c.* 1925 postcards, the display cases are nearly overflowing with objects, which are placed nearly on top of each other. By 1930, Stephen Pell had assembled an impressive collection of firearms, documents, maps, books, and other artifacts related to the 18th-century military history of the Lake Champlain and Lake George regions.

THE MUSEUM, FORT TICONDEROGA, N. Y.                                              10713

Like many old homes and hotels in the Lake Champlain region, Fort Ticonderoga has its share of ghost stories. One such story involved the fort's architect. In early May 1910, Alfred and Emily Bossom spent part of their honeymoon in the West Barracks. Late one evening, they looked out the window that faced the Southwest Bastion and saw what appeared to be an old man with a long white beard staring at them. Bossom wrote in his 1925 unpublished memoir, *The Restoration of Fort Ticonderoga,* "There was a rather dull moon outside—all the ingredients for the appropriate appearance of a ghost. Being a bridegroom and having to appear valiant, [I] went outside, down the wood steps, circled around the end of the building to see what the apparition consisted of, and there stood an old white angora goat." At that time, goats were being used to clear the brush around the old French line. In this *c.* 1910 postcard, the partially visible window behind the men is the one through which the Bossoms saw the ghostlike goat.

In early 1909, Stephen Pell began collecting 18th-century British, French, and American artillery to display at Fort Ticonderoga. This *c.* 1912 postcard shows part of the battery of 14 late-18th-century 24-pounder cannons that were presented to the fort through the efforts of British war secretary Lord Richard Haldane in 1911. Pell enlisted the aid of governments in Europe, the Caribbean, and Latin America to supplement the fort's growing artillery collection.

This *c.* 1934 postcard shows four 18th-century French bronze cannons mounted on the fort's South Terreplein. Fort Ticonderoga's collection of nearly 200 cannons, howitzers, and mortars, spanning the French and Indian War and Revolutionary War eras, is the largest of its type in the Western Hemisphere.

In the spring of 1914, work began on the restoration of the South Barracks. On July 31, work on the project was temporarily halted when Stephen Pell's brokerage firm went into receivership. This September 1914 photograph shows the extent of the restoration when the work was halted at that time. The western portion of the South Barracks had been excavated, and its walls were being stabilized. (Collection of the Fort Ticonderoga Museum.)

During 1915, the remainder of the South Barracks was excavated and its walls were raised to a height of about six feet. The barracks remained in this state until 1930, when its reconstruction resumed. This *c.* 1925 postcard shows the partially restored South Barracks and, behind it, the restored South Curtain Wall, which was restored *c.* 1917.

A woman standing on the Flag Bastion overlooking Lake Champlain is having her picture taken by a fellow tourist *c.* 1910. The Flag Bastion was restored in 1909 in time for the July 6 opening of the fort. To the left of the Flag Bastion are the remains of the South Battery Wall.

By 1916, the South Battery Wall was completed and the 24-pounder cannons received from Great Britain in 1911 were placed along it. An entranceway constructed in the South Battery Wall was called the Ethan Allen Gate in the belief that he and the other patriots who accompanied him passed through that portal when they assaulted the fort on May 10, 1775. The documentary evidence indicates that they approached the fort from a different direction.

The fort's powder magazine, located in the Southeast Bastion, was obliterated when the French blew it up in 1759 as they abandoned the fort. This *c.* 1905 postcard misidentifies an exposed fragment of the vaulted ceiling of the French ovens, located in the Northeast Bastion, as the entrance to the powder magazine. Some people believed that this opening was an entry to a secret passage that led from the fort to the shore of Lake Champlain.

By the mid-1920s, the foundation of the King's storehouse, destroyed by the exploding powder magazine in 1759, was excavated and its foundation walls were restored. The women in this *c.* 1925 postcard are heading toward the Northeast Bastion to view the restored French ovens. In the background to the left is the ruin of the fort's North Curtain Wall, and beyond the large tree is the ruin of the North, or Great, Demi-lune.

Bread was an important part of an 18th-century soldier's rations. The French ovens remained relatively intact, despite the ravages of time and pillagers. This *c.* 1905 postcard indicates that the only damage to the oven area is the collapse of a portion of a fireplace flue. The postcard misidentifies the area as the fort's powder magazine.

By the late 1920s, the French ovens were restored and open to the public. The ovens are the finest example of their type in North America. The opening in the ceiling on the right was for a chute through which firewood was slid for use in the ovens.

THE KING'S GARDEN, (1757), FORT TICONDEROGA, N. Y.

Around 1920, Marian Cruger Coffin (1876–1957), a pioneering female landscape architect, was hired by the Pell family to design a Colonial Revival–style formal garden behind the Pavilion. It was called *Le Jardin du Roi* (the King's Garden), a name derived from an 18th-century British map of the Garrison Grounds. After Sarah Pell's death in 1939, alterations were made to garden. The King's Garden has been restored to Coffin's original plan, and it is open to the public during the summer.

In 1937, internationally famous sculptor Anna Vaughn Hyatt Huntington (1876–1973), the wife of philanthropist Archer M. Huntington and a cousin of Stephen Pell, gave the Pell family the statue *The Young Diana*. The statue was placed in the reflecting pool in the middle of the King's Garden's focal point, the *tapis vert* (green carpet). The fort's East Curtain Wall can be seen in the background of this *c.* 1960 postcard.

The original Log House, constructed between 1909 and 1910, was a small building located to the west of the fort. Initially, it probably contained only a comfort station and a small souvenir stand. As shown above, by 1922, the Log House had been expanded to accommodate a constantly increasing number of tourists. The sign to the right of the door states, "Entrance to Fort Ticonderoga, Visitors Welcome, Admission to the Fortifications and Museum Fifty Cents, Proceeds used for Maintenance Fund, S.H.P. Pell, Open 8 am to 6 pm." By the 1930s, as seen in the postcard below, the size of the Log House had been increased again to include a restaurant. Today, the Log House continues to serve the same functions it did in the 1930s. (Above, collection of the Fort Ticonderoga Museum.)

The Fort Ticonderoga Fife & Drum Corps was founded in 1926 and played at the fort each summer season until the start of World War II. It was reactivated in 1973 and plays at the fort each July and August. The corps portrays the fifers and drummers of the Revolutionary War–era 1st New York Regiment. Pictured here are the corps playing at the 1939 World's Fair in New York City on Fort Ticonderoga Day, May 10, 1939. (Collection of the Fort Ticonderoga Museum.)

On July 9, 1927, John J. Pershing (1860–1948), general of the armies of the United States, and his family visited Fort Ticonderoga. Standing in front of the Log House are, from left to right, Stephen Pell (holding cane) and General Pershing (holding hat). On the extreme right, by the car, are Warren Pershing (General Pershing's son) and John H. G. Pell (Stephen Pell's son). (Collection of the Fort Ticonderoga Museum.)

ENTRANCE TO FORT TICONDEROGA. N. Y.

In the fall of 1927, Archer M. Huntington (1871–1955) gave the fort $10,000 (about $105,300 today) to restore the West Demi-lune. Archer was the son of Collis P. Huntington, one of the founders of the Central Pacific, Southern Pacific, and Chesapeake & Ohio Railroads. In the *c.* 1920 postcard, above, the stone-covered mound on the left is the ruin of the West Demi-lune. The restoration of the West Demi-lune was completed by August 1928, and cannons were mounted on it in 1929. A wooden bridge extending from the West Curtain Wall to the demilune was constructed in 1932. The restored triangular West Demi-lune is pictured in the *c.* 1930 postcard below.

SALLY PORT AND WEST DEMILUNE, FORT TICONDEROGA, NEW YORK

By 1930, the fort's collection of French and Indian War and Revolutionary War artifacts was too large to be exhibited entirely in the West Barracks. To provide more exhibition space, the restoration of the South Barracks, which had stopped in 1915, was resumed in the spring of 1930. These two photographs, dated July 6, 1930, are the only known images of the South Barracks taken during its restoration. In 1930, nearly $32,200 was spent to restore the barracks (about $361,000 today). An 18th-century French bush hammer found at the fort in the mid-1920s was used to finish the stones for the barracks' exterior walls. (Collection of the Fort Ticonderoga Museum.)

These *c.* 1940 postcards show the fort's exhibits on the second floor of the South Barracks. The mannequins are clothed in reproductions of French, British, and American uniforms of the French and Indian War, the American Revolution, and the War of 1812. The mannequins were eventually removed from display because visitors disfigured them by taking buttons and small pieces of clothing as souvenirs.

123

A solitary visitor inspects a wall of the North, or Great, Demi-lune in this *c.* 1885 view looking east. The mound of rubble behind the visitor, to the left, contains the fort's North Curtain Wall. Partially visible in the background behind the north curtain wall is a chimney of the West Barracks. (Collection of the Fort Ticonderoga Museum.)

The restoration of the North, or Great, Demi-lune was begun in 1929 and completed in 1930. During the excavating, several large rooms were discovered. These rooms were once thought to be dungeons because their window sills had holes that may have been for iron bars. There is no credible evidence indicating the existence of a dungeon there.

AEROPLANE VIEW OF FORT TICONDEROGA, N. Y.

A significant amount of restoration work was completed in the 1925–1931 period. In the 1925 aerial view of the fort shown in the *c.* 1926 postcard above, only the West Barracks and the Northwest and Southwest Bastions had been restored. By late 1931, as shown in the postcard below, the South Barracks and the West and North Demi-lunes had been restored. In addition, work had begun on the restoration of the North Curtain Wall and North Terreplein. The walls of the Northwest and Southwest Bastions, to the right and left of the West Barracks, had been raised to accommodate the fort's growing collection of 18th-century artillery.

FORT TICONDEROGA, N. Y. — AIRPLANE VIEW FROM THE EAST

The restoration of the North Terreplein and North Curtain Wall, on the right in this *c.* 1960 postcard, was started in 1930 and was completed in 1933. Howland Pell provided a portion of the funds required for its restoration in memory of his son H. Gallatin Pell. Friends of Gallatin Pell provided additional funding by subscribing $25 per person (about $275 today) toward the cost of the project.

This *c.* 1940 photograph shows the restoration of the East Terreplein, the East Curtain Wall, and the Northeast Bastion. These projects were the last major restorations made inside the fort in the 20th century. When these projects were completed, visitors could walk completely around the circumference of the fort on its exterior walls for the first time since 1759. (Collection of the Fort Ticonderoga Museum.)

There is a tradition of 20th-century pottery making at Fort Ticonderoga. Sometime between 1909 and 1924, the Pell family established the Fort Ticonderoga Pottery Works on the Garrison Grounds. On January 2, 1925, a fire destroyed the Fort Ticonderoga Pottery Works. Around 1930, Stephen Pell invited potter Henry Graack Jr., then living in New York City, to come to the fort during the summer months and make replicas of Indian pottery to sell to the tourists. Graack pottery made at the fort was stamped "Fort Ticonderoga" on its bottom. Graack pottery was sold in the small log cabin, shown above, that was adjacent to the fort's Log House. By the 1950s, Graack had stopped making pottery at the fort, and the log cabin was converted into the Fort Ticonderoga post office, shown below, where visitors could get stamps and mail the souvenir postcards they purchased at the Log House. Eventually, the log cabin was moved farther west along the Fort Road, and today it serves as the headquarters of the Fort Ticonderoga Fife & Drum Corps. (Above, collection of the Fort Ticonderoga Museum.)

*Fort Ticonderoga Ruins.* **1902**

Fort Ticonderoga was designated a National Historic Landmark in 1960 and was one of the first historic sites to be listed on the National Register of Historic Places. The restoration of Fort Ticonderoga has been a tremendous undertaking, as can be seen by comparing the *c.* 1902 postcard above with the *c.* 1965 postcard below. These postcards provide before and after views of the same section of the fort. The restored fort is a tribute to the thousands of soldiers who served there, as well as to the generations of generous friends who have contributed their money and time to continue the work started by Stephen and Sarah Pell. This work continues into the 21st century. By 2009, the 100th anniversary of the start of the restoration of the fort, the Mars Education Center will be constructed on site of King's storehouse. You are invited to enlist in this effort by joining the Friends of Fort Ticonderoga. For more information, visit the fort's Web site at www.fort-ticonderoga.org.